MW01034308

RAIN OF RUIN

RAIN OF RUIN

Tokyo, Hiroshima, and the Surrender of Japan

Richard Overy

W. W. NORTON & COMPANY
Independent Publishers Since 1923

For information about permission to reproduce selections from
this book, write to Permissions, W. W. Norton & Company, Inc.,
500 Fifth Avenue, New York, NY 10110

For information about special discounts for bulk purchases, please
contact W. W. Norton Special Sales at specialsales@wwnorton.com or
800-233-4830

Manufacturing by Lakeside Book Company
Production manager: Lauren Abbate

ISBN 978-1-324-10530-5

W. W. Norton & Company, Inc.
500 Fifth Avenue, New York, NY 10110
www.wwnorton.com

W. W. Norton & Company Ltd.
15 Carlisle Street, London W1D 3BS

10 9 8 7 6 5 4 3 2 1

CONTENTS

Operations Against Japan, June 1944 – September 1945

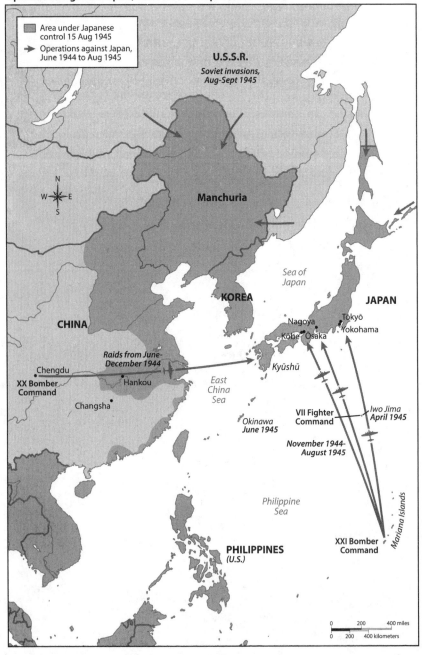

The Bombing of Mainland Japan, November 1944 – August 1945

B29 targets in Japan
- Atomic bomb targets
- Main fire bomb targets
- Secondary fire bomb targets
- U.S. mine-laying sites

Sakhalin

U.S.S.R.

Manchuria

Hokkaidō

N
W — E
S

Sea of Japan

KOREA

JAPAN

Honshū

Hiroshima
Aug 6

Kōbe · Kyoto

Nagoya

Tōkyō

Kawasaki
Yokohama

Ōsaka

Shikoku

PACIFIC OCEAN

XXI Bomber Command
(from Marianas)

XXI Bomber Command
(from Marianas)

VII Fighter Command
(from Iwo Jima)

Nagasaki
Aug 9

Kyūshū

East China Sea

0   50   100 miles
0   50   100 kilometers

"It Will Be All-Out"

If war with the Japanese does come, we'll fight mercilessly.
Flying Fortresses will be dispatched immediately to
set the paper cities of Japan on fire. There won't be any
hesitation about bombing civilians—it will be all-out.

—PRESS CONFERENCE OF GENERAL

MARSHALL, NOVEMBER 15, 1941[1]

WHEN GEORGE MARSHALL, U.S. ARMY CHIEF OF STAFF,
made his views known to a small group of prominent American
journalists just weeks before Pearl Harbor, there was no prospect
that the Boeing B-17 "Flying Fortress" could reach any target in the
Japanese home islands. The motives for such a piece of bravado are
difficult to fathom, unless Marshall hoped that a more indiscreet
member of his small audience would let Japanese leaders understand
the threat they faced if they risked war. Bombing of civilians was
widely condemned by American opinion, including President
Roosevelt, Marshall's titular commander in chief. The reference to

"paper cities" showed a casual racism common to many Westerners when they confronted Japan's apparently exotic culture. As it turned out, bombing of Japanese cities, nearly all of them, could happen only after almost four years of a bitterly fought struggle across the South and Central Pacific. Marshall's claim that the bombing would be "all-out" was the one promise redeemed. In 1945, Japan experienced the three most deadly bombing attacks of the war—on Tokyo, Hiroshima, and Nagasaki. Almost two-thirds of Japan's "paper cities" were destroyed by fire and blast, the "rain of ruin" promised by President Truman in August 1945. Why that happened and with what consequences is the subject of this short book.

American military leaders had long thought about how Japan might be defeated if a Pacific war ever materialized between the two major naval powers in the region. Bombing was late on the scene because no available airplane could reach Japan from war-torn China or the southern Pacific until the advent of the B-29 "Superfortress" in summer 1944. It was inevitable, however, given the large-scale commitment to strategic bombing in the European theater, that the Army Air Forces would plan to degrade the Japanese war effort as they were doing against Germany. Strategic bombing was a central element in the Western strategic armory—where it was largely absent for its Soviet ally—because waging this kind of indirect, economic warfare matched a strategic conception that saw pressure on the enemy home front as a legitimate and effective use of air power. The British had pursued this strategy ruthlessly in Europe and hoped to join the American air forces for the campaign against Japan once Hitler was defeated. The result for Japan was the firebombing campaign from March to August 1945 and the climactic nuclear attacks in the penultimate week of the Pacific war. These are often treated as different subjects, but they were complementary operations directed at destroying Japan's cities and will be treated as such in what follows. The British Mission to Japan, whose purpose was to compile a report on the bombing, observed the link between the two: "the incendiary raids of March undoubtedly paved the way for the collapse of morale that followed the atomic bombs." Japanese peace feelers in June 1945, the report continued, followed these raids, "and the atomic bombs of August ripened but did not plant them."[2]

The United States Army Air Forces, which carried out both conventional and nuclear raids, liked to think that air power had delivered the Japanese surrender a few days after the bombing of Hiroshima, and that has remained a conclusion endorsed by many historians. If there were ethical issues raised, the answer was military necessity against a savage enemy: bombing Japan into surrender saved untold numbers of American lives, an outcome that was regarded then and now as a higher moral imperative than concern for hundreds of thousands of Japanese civilians. "But to worry about the *morality* of what we doing—Nuts," announced Curtis LeMay, commander of the bombing campaign, twenty years after the event. "If we accomplished the job in any given battle," he continued, "without exterminating too many of our own folks, we considered that we'd had a pretty good day."[3] Those were, and have remained, central arguments on one side of the postwar debate over the effectiveness and morality of the bombing campaign.

With the passage of time, these assumptions about the bombing seem much less clear-cut, raising as many questions as they answer and spawning a vast historical literature. Why did the American air forces adopt a strategy of indiscriminate firebombing of Japanese cities when the same air forces commanders in Europe had been critical of British "area bombing" of Germany with incendiaries designed to burn down city centers? What prompted the development of nuclear weapons and secured the decision for their use? Did the bombing, both conventional and atomic, provoke the Japanese surrender or are there other explanations that put the bombing into a context where the claims of air power have to be scaled down? Were the nuclear weapons designed as a cynical demonstration of American power and technical accomplishment to intimidate the Soviet Union as the two states rapidly approached the Cold War confrontation? Finally, the question that remains open to this day: Was the bombing morally justified and justifiable or an unpunished war crime? To each of these questions there have been a great many answers. No single subject in the history of the United States war effort has prompted so much historical, political, and philosophical writing. No set of surviving records has been subjected to so much close forensic scrutiny.

The object of this short book is to set out these issues clearly and to indicate how they might be answered with what we now know eighty years after the event. Two elements are introduced here to expand what is often a very American narrative. First, the Japanese side of the history is now much better known than it was a generation ago and is integrated as fully as possible in the discussion of both kinds of bombing and their effects on Japan's leadership and wider population. Understanding the Japanese view of surrender shows why it was so difficult to achieve—indeed it was never called a surrender but "termination of the war." Second, there is more here from the British side of the history, because Britain was also a major belligerent in the war against Japan but often overlooked in accounts of Japanese defeat because British forces were bogged down in Southeast Asia. Both Winston Churchill and Harry S. Truman gave the nod to the use of the two atomic bombs. British bomber squadrons were poised to arrive in the Pacific just at the point at which Japan capitulated. A team of top British scientists arrived at Los Alamos in 1944 to help engineer the bombs, but they have often been airbrushed out of the narrative as if they contributed nothing of significance.[4]

The text that follows owes a good deal to the wealth of current scholarship, to which I am very much indebted. The issues raised in this history are often presented in terms of judging the past, particularly in this case where writers on the one hand think that it would have been better morally not to firebomb Tokyo or to submit Hiroshima and Nagasaki to atomic attacks, and writers on the other hand assume that the Japanese deserved what they got for failing to give up. The object in this book is not to judge the past but to try to understand it better in its own terms, as all good history should. Living today in a renewed age of crisis, in which civilian populations are once again subjected to indiscriminate bombardment, there are certainly lessons to be learned from this history.

Richard Overy
FEBRUARY 2024

RAIN OF RUIN

CHAPTER 1

Defeat of Japan

Plan Orange: General Concept: Phase III. "A campaign
directed towards the isolation of Japan through
control of all waters surrounding Japan, through the
equivalent of blockade operations, and through the
capture and occupation of all outlying Japanese islands,
intensified by an air war over Japanese territory."

—PLAN ORANGE, GENERAL CONCEPT, 1923[1]

IN 1906, THE AMERICAN JOINT ARMY AND NAVY BOARD
authorized limited contingency planning for a possible future war
with Japan, now a potential rival in the Pacific after Japan's defeat
of Russia in 1905. The putative enemy was code-named "Orange";
the United States bore the color "Blue." From then until the final
years of the Second World War, American navy and army planners
thought about the most effective ways to defeat Japan. The plan
was modified as time went by, but the 1923 version, cited above,

prompted by sudden fear that Japan might threaten the Philippines, established the main lines to be pursued if conflict did break out: a state of siege established by naval blockade, and then, after the capture of nearby islands, an air war against the Japanese homeland. Although the eventual war fought between 1941 and 1945 was larger and longer than the one envisaged in Plan Orange, the final defeat of Japan followed very closely the speculative scenario drafted in 1923.

The place of air power in Plan Orange was a novelty introduced after the First World War, during which a small United States air force had participated in the final year of fighting under the control of the Army Expeditionary Force. Despite the army's hostility to the idea of independent air strategy, Plan Orange was updated to a full war plan in 1928 to include "intensive air attacks" designed to wreck the Japanese economy from bases captured in the island chains near to Japan. This was assumed to be an essential component of any blockade strategy, and it was designed to make a ground invasion of the Japanese home islands unnecessary. The planners who worked on Plan Orange assumed throughout the interwar years that Japan itself was "almost invulnerable" to amphibious assault because of the problems of supply across the Pacific and the ferocious resistance likely to be met. When U.S. Army planners were asked to speculate about possible invasion sites, they reluctantly suggested the southern Japanese island of Kyūshū and the Tokyo plain on the main island of Honshū, the very same destinations later chosen in 1945 when the U.S. Army was at last able to plan a real invasion. The bombing strategy was not updated again throughout the 1930s, but it remained in place to be absorbed by fresh strategic plans drawn up between 1939 and 1941 to cope with multiple threats.[2] The so-called Rainbow Plans (merging the different color codes used in United States contingency planning) included Rainbow Plan 3, essentially a version of Plan Orange. Rainbow 5 came to be preferred for a possible war in Europe first, which seemed a more likely possibility, but plans for a war with Japan continued to rely on the outlines prepared years before.

More threatened by the prospect of Japanese ambitions in East Asia and the South Pacific was the British Empire. After the abrogation of the 1902 Anglo-Japanese Alliance in 1922, relations between the two naval empires deteriorated. British hopes rested on naval power. In the early 1920s, it was decided to build a major naval base at Singapore, which would serve as a deterrence to Japan and protection for the Asian empire. It was hoped that the sight of a major base, to be reinforced swiftly by units of the Royal Navy Home and Mediterranean Fleets in the event of a crisis, would be enough to keep Japan from its own imperial adventures. Like Plan Orange, British thinking from the early 1920s onward focused on the possibility of long-distance blockade, cutting Japanese trade from the Indian Ocean or across the South Pacific by using a global network of checkpoints to prevent imports reaching Japan. Invasion of the Japanese home islands was ruled out, as it was by the U.S. Navy, as beyond strategic reach. The "Singapore Strategy," fixed by 1923, remained the center point of British plans for a war with Japan and defense of the empire.[3] The Singapore base was completed at great cost by 1938, its colossal main guns famously pointing out to sea at the expense of any defense from attack mounted against Singapore Island from the rear. As relations with Japan reached a crisis point in 1940 and 1941, the British tried to get the United States to share the "Singapore Strategy" by basing the U.S. Pacific Fleet there, but the Americans eventually rejected a plan that would leave the eastern Pacific completely exposed while protecting chiefly the British Empire.[4] Later, in May 1941, British planners expressed the hope that the United States might still serve British interests by threatening to bomb Japanese cities. Royal Air Force plans for the bombing of Japan did not materialize until late 1943, once the American pursuit of the equivalent of Plan Orange in the Pacific promised to bring air bases within range of the home islands. In the end, the RAF arrived too late in 1945 to participate. Intensive air bombardment, fixed in United States planning from at least 1928, remained an American monopoly.

The reality in the interwar years differed widely from the thinking in Plan Orange. The U.S. Army was hostile to the idea that its Air Service (renamed the Army Air Corps in 1926) would engage in anything other than support for the land war or the defense of the continental United States. In 1926, the U.S. War Department dictated that air forces were created "to aid the ground forces to gain decisive success."[5] In the 1930s, any suggestion that the Army Air Corps might contribute its own air strategy based on long-range bombing was suppressed. In 1932, the air corps possessed only ninety-two light bombers. The firmest opponent of independent air force operations was the U.S. Army assistant chief of staff in the mid-1930s, Brig. Gen. Stanley Embick. Aircraft, he claimed, not altogether wrongly, "cannot occupy nor control permanently either land or sea areas, they are impotent and helpless in flight. . . . They are fragile, vulnerable to the smallest missile, inoperable in bad weather, and exceedingly costly."[6] When the army established a small GHQ Air Force in 1935, its purpose was to supply a reserve of aircraft to support army operations and to counter attacks from an enemy air force. Strategic air power did not appear in any army plans in the late 1930s, while the navy wanted long-range aircraft under naval control for the coastal defense of the Western Hemisphere. The one army aircraft that had the range to play a strategic role, the Boeing B-17 four-engine bomber, produced in prototype in 1935 to an air corps specification, was scrapped by the War Department in late 1938 in favor of larger numbers of battlefield bombers for army support.[7] A few early production models of the B-17 remained, but there was effectively no air component remotely capable of bombing Japan or indeed anywhere else. Strategic air power in the United States survived by the very slenderest of margins.

The absence of a bomber force did not prevent Army Air Corps officers from developing the doctrine for bombing operations if they should ever become a possibility. The outspoken William "Billy" Mitchell, assistant chief of the Army Air Service in the mid-1920s, developed the idea of bombing an enemy's "vital centers"— transport, industry, cities—by day and by night using a mix of high-explosive bombs, incendiaries, and poison gas. Like the Italian air strategist Giulio Douhet, whose *Il dominio dell'aria* [*Command of the Air*] appeared in 1921, Mitchell thought an air campaign might end a war on its own.[8] Mitchell's influence was profound. American airmen came to accept that "bombardment is the basic arm," even when the army told them otherwise. The commander of the GHQ Air Force in 1935, Maj. Gen. Frank Andrews, paid lip service to the doctrine of ground support while privately encouraging the doctrine of independent air operations against factories, oil refineries, power plants, and urban centers of population.[9] His views were elaborated by a generation of young officers at the Air Corps Tactical School (who later served in senior commands in the Second World War) attracted by the idea that air power could prove itself only by independent campaigns against an enemy's "national web" or "social body." Assaulting the home front, according to one of the tactical school's lectures, meant attacking "where the enemy is weakest"; the economic network and the fabric of enemy society were the Achilles' heel of any belligerent power.[10] Japan as a putative enemy was regarded as particularly vulnerable, "an ideal objective for air attack," as one student paper claimed. In September 1939, Lt. Col. Carl Spaatz, later in summer 1945 overall commander of strategic air forces in the Pacific, proposed to the Army Air Corps chief of staff, Gen. Henry "Hap" Arnold, a plan for an air offensive against Japan that would make invasion unnecessary and produce results more rapidly than blockade.[11] The doctrinal shape of the future bombing campaign against Japan was already developed long before there was any capability of achieving it.

The air corps was rescued from the prejudices of the army by President Franklin Roosevelt. After the Munich Conference in late September 1938, Roosevelt told his cabinet that bombing of Germany might have prevented capitulation to Hitler's demands. In January 1939, he reversed the War Department's decision to scrap the B-17 by calling for a program of heavy bombers. In March 1939, he established an Air Board, which came out strongly in favor of a major program of B-17 production. The board also approved the development of a larger aircraft, with long range and heavy payload, which allowed Boeing to begin development on what became the B-29 very heavy bomber, used for the later bombardment of Japan.[12] Although the president appealed in early September 1939 to the belligerent powers not to bomb undefended civilians, he regularly supported the development of American bombing capability in the years that followed. The same month, Roosevelt appointed a new army chief of staff, Gen. George Marshall, who shared his view of air-power potential. Marshall helped draw up new regulations for the exercise of air power. Air forces now enjoyed the strategic function of defeating an enemy through "the destruction of his means of waging war or by overcoming his will to resist," both of which might be achieved by the exercise of independent air campaigns. "Air power," wrote Marshall, "is based upon the offensive fire power of the bombardment aeroplane."[13] By 1940, the air corps was now in a position to begin gathering intelligence for a possible air offensive against the most likely enemies—Germany, Italy, and Japan, but also the Soviet Union.

WHEN WAR WITH JAPAN broke out on December 7, 1941, with the Japanese aircraft carrier raid on the naval base at Pearl Harbor, there was still no possibility of a bombing campaign against the home islands of Japan. Any potential air bases in the Pacific were swiftly overrun by the Japanese armed forces as they captured the Philippines, Guam, Wake Island, Malaya, the Dutch East Indies, and a string of South Pacific islands. The only available long-range bomber, the B-17, lacked the range to reach Japanese industrial cities even if the bases had been saved. Priority was given to the war in Europe against the strong objections of the U.S. Navy, and it was here that the first American bombing offensive was established with the posting of the Eighth Air Force to British bases in 1942. The Pacific war became divided between the U.S. Army and U.S. Navy, the former campaigning in the Southwest Pacific toward the recapture of the Philippines under Gen. Douglas MacArthur, the latter under Adm. Chester Nimitz undertaking the capture of a string of islands across the Central Pacific, a strategy anticipated in Plan Orange. The result was to leave the Army Air Forces (successor in 1941 to the Army Air Corps) with no prospect of a strategic role in the Pacific until there were bases near enough to Japan and an aircraft with a sufficient range to reach Japanese targets. Instead, the air forces had to be content with tactical support of MacArthur's campaigns, while naval aviation supported the advance through the Pacific islands. Although there was a major bombing offensive in Europe, Arnold, now a member of the American Joint Chiefs of Staff, chafed at the bit that the air forces could not play a significant role against an enemy understood to be uniquely vulnerable to assault from the air.

Marshall's assurance in November 1941 that Japanese cities would be bombed "all-out" was a strategic fantasy when war came a month later. The order sent out only hours after the Pearl Harbor attack to undertake "unrestricted air and submarine warfare against Japan" was hope rather than expectation.[14] This did not deter Arnold from authorizing the preparation of target folders on Japanese cities as early as February 1942.[15] Arnold fretted over the development of the B-29, the only aircraft with the necessary range, whose innovative engineering was plagued with design and development problems. Not the least of those was the Wright R3350 engine, which regularly caught fire, killing Boeing's chief test pilot on the B-29 prototype's second flight. Production of the engines was constantly interrupted by design changes—a total of 6,247 during the war—and by sudden alterations in the air force production program, which left factories having to retool at short notice.[16] Without the aircraft arriving on time and in quantity, strategic air power in the Pacific war was not a possibility, yet it remained a central ambition for an air force hoping to break away from the overall control of the army to establish its independence. The devastating effect that independent strategic bombing on its own might have was regularly used as a justification for greater air force autonomy. Arnold told the Territorial Committee, set up in 1943 by the State Department to discuss the future of Japan and its empire after the war, that "ultimately our aerial operations in the Pacific must call for bombing Japan with complete havoc—bombing to assure the total destruction of the enemy on his own soil."[17]

Roosevelt shared Arnold's impatience. The Doolittle Raid on Tokyo on April 18, 1942—a handful of aircraft launched from an aircraft carrier, under the command of the aeronautical pioneer Lt. Col. James Doolittle—was a token gesture but not enough to satisfy the president. Roosevelt had been briefly persuaded by a proposal sent to him in February 1942 to use bats to carry small incendiary bombs to Japanese towns, where they would find "dark crevices" to nestle in, starting fires inaccessible to the fire services. This fanciful project continued to be funded down to March 1944. Less favor was shown to a later proposal to create artificial floating islands from which 1,000 bombers could attack Japan's cities.[18] The hope that Japan might be bombed from bases in Siberia foundered on Soviet rejection of an operation that not only violated the neutrality pact signed with Japan in April 1941 but also invited numerous logistic and security problems.

Not until spring 1943, after the end of the Battle of Guadalcanal and the first retreat of Japanese forces, did the Army Air Forces begin planning for the possible future bombing of Japan, even though thousands of miles of ocean still separated the nearest airfields from the Japanese home islands. By this stage, Roosevelt had already taken two decisions that were to have fundamental significance in shaping the last stages of the war against Japan. First, in December 1941, he approved an American research program to investigate the possibility of an atomic bomb, followed in June 1942 by authorization of a project under army control to try to produce one (later in September 1944 he agreed with Winston Churchill in a meeting at the president's Hyde Park estate that the bomb, now a feasible product, might "after mature consideration" be used against Japan).[19] Second, in January 1943, after discussion with State Department officials and with Churchill's casual approval, he announced at a press conference concluding the Anglo-American Casablanca Conference that the three Axis states would have to surrender unconditionally. Roosevelt did not live to see the fruit of these two decisions, but he never wavered from either of them.

Roosevelt also intervened in the debate about how or when the conventional bombing of Japan might be possible. Eager to support the Chinese war effort more directly, he shifted the focus of a possible bombing campaign against targets in the Japanese Empire from bases in China. In early March 1943, he wrote to Marshall that not enough attention had been paid at the Casablanca Conference—convened to agree upon Anglo-American high-level strategy—to the issue of attrition against Japan by air action from China, including "the occasional bombing of Japanese cities."[20] Marshall summarized the arguments for the Joint Chiefs of Staff some days later for a highly destructive campaign against Japanese targets from Chinese bases, including "Japan proper," which would "seriously complicate" Japan's war effort.[21] The same month Arnold asked the American Committee of Operation Analysts, set up for the war in Europe, to begin discussion on Japanese priority targets. By May 1943, the Army Air Forces' Air Warfare Plans Division began work on the target requirements for a bombing campaign to be launched against Japanese targets from bases in China, though the planners hoped the campaign could ultimately be conducted from island bases captured in the Pacific.[22]

The China option was approved by Roosevelt and Churchill when they met at the Inter-Allied Conference in Quebec in August 1943 (code-named Quadrant). Neither of them fully appreciated the strategic challenge such a decision entailed, though they may well have been misled by Arnold, who made a lurid presentation at the conference of the destruction and level of casualty a bombing campaign would create. This was an argument already familiar to Churchill from the regular promises by Air Marshal Arthur Harris, commander of RAF Bomber Command, that city bombing would soon knock Germany out of the war. In November, Roosevelt wrote to Churchill that the project for heavy bombing from China was under way and asked him to help get bases constructed in India from which supplies could be flown to the Chengdu area of China, northwest of the Chinese capital Chongqing, from which the new heavy bombers would launch their operations. "This is," he wrote, "a bold and entirely feasible project" that would cripple Japanese military power "and hasten the victory of our forces in Asia." The request was passed on to the British Supreme Commander Southeast Asia, Lord Louis Mountbatten, who replied that if the United States supplied the equipment, the bases could be completed by May 1944.[23] A few weeks later, at the Cairo Conference between Roosevelt, Churchill, and the Chinese leader, Marshal Chiang Kai-shek, the American Joint Planning Staff elaborated its ideas about a bombing campaign launched initially from China, but once the Mariana Islands were captured, from Guam, Saipan, and Tinian. The air forces member on the Joint Planning Staff, Haywood Hansell, suggested that bombing might be decisive in the defeat of Japan, a possibility that the army and navy planners were reluctant to accept but which Hansell inserted surreptitiously in the final staff report. The Combined Chiefs of Staff approved on December 2, 1943, a strategy in which invasion of the home islands might not be necessary if Japan could be defeated "by sea and air blockade and an intensive air bombardment," the main thrust of the original Plan Orange.[24]

The intention to bomb Japanese targets in China, Manchuria, and the home islands was still anything but feasible. Japan controlled a vast area of northern and eastern China so that bombing of Japan from Chinese bases would mean long-range operations at the limit of the B-29's radius. Nevertheless, Arnold was keen to exploit the opportunity provided by Roosevelt to employ the B-29 in operations even before its technical teething troubles had been eliminated. Both men were aware that American public opinion, informed about the new "super bomber," was impatient to see bombs dropped on Japan, but aspiration ran far ahead of capability. A new air force was activated for the purpose on November 20, 1943, the Twentieth (it ought to have been the Sixteenth, but twenty was thought to be a more memorable number), commanded by Brig. Gen. Kenneth Wolfe but under the area command in China of the acerbic Gen. Joseph "Vinegar Joe" Stilwell, American adviser to Chiang Kai-shek.* To avoid the danger that the B-29s might be side-

---

* The Twentieth Air Force, like the other wartime U.S. air forces, was made up not only of the Twentieth Bomber Command but also a headquarters section, a service section, and a dedicated fighter force. Arnold commanded the Twenti-

tracked to support the tactical needs of the army, Arnold took the unusual step in April 1944 of placing the Twentieth directly under his control in Washington, where the headquarters operated many thousands of miles away from the site of operations. The bombing campaign, first code-named Operation Twilight for Stilwell's plan to operate from bases around Changsha in south-central China, was renamed Matterhorn when Chengdu in western China, further from the Japanese area of occupation, became the favored site. The operation worked to the same concept and wording as the Casablanca Directive to the bomber forces in Europe drawn up earlier in the year: "the progressive destruction and dislocation of the Japanese military, industrial, and economic systems, and the undermining of the morale of the Japanese people to the point where their capacity for armed resistance is fatally weakened." Stilwell was given a list of priority targets to achieve these aims, drawn up by the Committee of Operation Analysts and the Air War Plans Division. The emphasis was on the precision bombing of key industrial locations to match United States practice in the European bombing war. The priority targets were the coke ovens that fed Japan's steel industry in Manchuria, Korea, and Japan, the main Japanese shipping centers, and the Japanese aeronautical industry. The list also included Japanese "industrial and urban areas," a target borrowed from British practice in the European air war, and one that eventually opened the way to the massive urban destruction meted out to Japan in 1945.[25]

Nothing could be done until the bases at Kharagpur (near Calcutta) and in Chengdu were completed and the necessary stores and fuel in place. The RAF hoped to be able to join the campaign from India only later but expected there to be a "combined effort" once Germany was defeated.[26] In the interim, the British authorities in India relied on the United States to supply most of the equipment

---

eth Air Force, but Wolfe commanded the Twentieth Bomber Command under Arnold's overall direction.

for the new bases. The plan was to bring the B-29s to India, fly them over the Himalayas to China (a route known as "the Hump"), and there to supply them by air with oil, bombs, and stores flown over the same long route by 2,000 converted Consolidated B-24 bombers. But the B-24s could not be spared from the European war, and the B-29s were left to provide their own supply. The Combined Logistics Committee and the Joint War Plans Committee both rejected the plan as unworkable, but Arnold with Roosevelt's backing persisted. The result was that eight flights across the Hump by the B-29s were needed to supply just one B-29 operation.[27] For every seven gallons of fuel expended in the supply effort, only one gallon was available for the bombers, a logistic outcome that made no operational sense. It was calculated that during the first nine months of B-29 deployment to Asia, only 14 percent of flights were actually directed at the enemy. The bases prepared around Chengdu had crude runways, too short for the heavy bombers to take off and land safely, poor facilities for the crew, many of whom were short of training time on the new aircraft, and a shortage of engineering staff to cope with the regular technical problems plaguing the B-29 engines. By early 1944, only sixteen B-29s were operational out of ninety-seven delivered by the Boeing factories, though eventually 3,760 would be produced at a final cost of almost $4 billion. The first aircraft available after extensive modification were sent on to India in March along a complex route from bases in Kansas through Newfoundland, Morocco, Egypt, and Karachi. By May, 130 had reached India, and after flying on to China they undertook on June 5, 1944, the first raid from Chengdu bases against the railway yards in Bangkok, capital of Thailand. Of the ninety-eight bombers sent off, only eighteen found the target, and five of the expensive aircraft were lost through mechanical causes.[28] It proved an inauspicious birth for a campaign supposed to cripple the Japanese military and economic war effort.

The same month the Japanese Army launched a major land campaign against the American air bases in eastern China, Operation Ichi-Gō. The operation succeeded in overrunning six American bases used by the tactical air force under Gen. Claire Chennault in the Changsha area scheduled initially for the bombers, but progress along the Yangtze toward Chengdu was brought to a halt. Instead, Japanese aircraft occasionally bombed the B-29 bases, destroying a small number of aircraft, but the threat remained that the area might be subject to what the Joint Intelligence Committee in an earlier warning had called "a strong raiding column."[29] Japanese air and antiaircraft defenses against the B-29 were limited. There were occasional hits by antiaircraft fire against planes flying at very high altitude (about 30,000 feet) and only intermittent fighter success. Japanese aircraft, scant in number in mainland China, lacked the firepower and speed to destroy the B-29s and in most cases could not fly high enough to engage in combat at altitude. At night, the few Japanese night fighters, chiefly the more effective Kawasaki Ki-45 "Dragon Killer," lacked nighttime radar to locate aircraft away from searchlight illumination. By December 1944, some Japanese pilots resorted to ramming oncoming bombers in line with the official approval of suicide tactics.

For most of the campaign from China, B-29 losses were caused more often by atrocious weather conditions or mechanical failure. The first raid against Japan was undertaken on June 15, 1944, against the coke ovens of the iron and steel works at Yawata on the island of Kyūshū. Flying at night in loose formation, the aircraft made a round trip of 3,200 miles. Out of sixty-three B-29s taking off, forty-seven located the target, but the damage they caused was minimal. Of the seven aircraft lost, only one was to enemy action. In a further raid against Yawata on August 20, Japanese resistance was heavier, but out of fourteen bombers lost, only four were felled in combat.[30] Out of 125 losses of B-29s for the Twentieth Bomber Command, 96 were to noncombat causes, chiefly the persistent problem that the engines regularly caught fire and burned through the wing. Nor were the overall statistics on sorties flown and bombs dropped impressive by the standards expected from the new force. Only 11,244 tons of bombs were dropped in 3,058 sorties (6.7 percent of the bomb tonnage later dropped on Japanese targets) over the ten months from June 1944 to March 1945, when the Twentieth Bomber Command was deactivated.[31]

Arnold remained frustrated with results from the China operations, which in the end contributed very little to the eventual defeat of Japan. By mid-1944, the American joint chiefs had decided that invasion of the home islands was the most probable option once the island chains on the approach to Japan had been captured. At the Inter-Allied Conference in Quebec in September 1944 (code-named Octagon), the Combined Chiefs of Staff agreed to an integrated strategy of blockade, bombing, and invasion. Intensive air bombardment was to be part of the campaign, and perhaps the involvement of the Soviet Union if Joseph Stalin decided to abrogate the pact with Japan, but based on the record from China, the effectiveness of air power in the final defeat of the enemy was still in the balance. Operation Matterhorn was continued as much for political reasons as for military. Arnold wanted to demonstrate the power of strategic air operations as a prelude to air force independence; Roosevelt wanted to redeem his promises to Chiang Kai-shek of American assistance; and the early bombing was designed for psychological effect on the home population in Japan, whose previous inviolability was now punctured.

For the Twentieth Bomber Command, the campaign was a rude awakening to the gap between political incentive and operational reality. When the young Maj. Gen. Curtis LeMay was sent from the Eighth Air Force in Europe to take over the command in August 1944, he later recalled his initial reaction to "an utterly absurd logistic basis . . . like something out of the *Wizard of Oz*."[32] In his memoirs he complained that "our entire Nation howled like a pack of wolves for an attack on the Japanese homeland," but "Folks were given an impossible task to perform."[33] On his arrival at Chengdu, he told the Washington headquarters that he found the Twentieth to be "very poor as a combat outfit. . . . We have no business operating B-29s out of here any longer than is necessary."[34] He improved training regimes, tried to increase bomb loads, which were little more than could be carried by the smaller B-17, and sought to raise morale among crews who disliked the conditions and the danger in flying an aircraft that was more likely to kill them than the enemy. After a handful of missions with poor results against targets in Manchuria and Kyūshū, from January to March 1945 the Twentieth Bomber Command flew twenty raids from the Kharagpur bases in India against targets in Southeast Asia until its operations were wound up.[35] Yet only six months later, the B-29s had laid waste to half of Japan's urban area and dropped on Hiroshima and Nagasaki two atomic bombs. It proved to be a short but fateful learning curve.

CHAPTER 2

American "Area Bombing"

Over half of Tokyo is now gone. The three Tokyo incendiary
operations have certainly been among the most effective
in the entire history of bombing. Keep up the good work.

—LAURIS NORSTAD TO CURTIS LEMAY, APRIL 1945[1]

BY THE TIME BRIG. GEN. LAURIS NORSTAD WROTE TO
Curtis LeMay in April 1945, a remarkable 40 percent of the Japanese
capital had been quite literally burned to the ground. Norstad was
chief of staff of the Twentieth Air Force, and in the absence of
Henry Arnold, who was convalescing from a heart attack, he was
the effective overall commander in Washington. Nothing about the
history of the Twentieth Air Force in China indicated that within
months the Army Air Forces would switch from precision bombing
of industrial targets at high altitude to nighttime low-altitude raids
to burn down residential city centers deliberately. Norstad was an
advocate of the idea that incendiary bombing might maximize what

the bombers could achieve and pressed commanders to experiment with what amounted to American "area bombing," the name given to the mass raids on German cities carried out by RAF Bomber Command with growing intensity from 1941 onward. American skepticism of the strategic wisdom of area bombing in the European air campaign was set aside when confronted with the urgent need to force Japan to end the war.

The transformation of American air force strategy has remained one of the central areas of debate on the last months of the Pacific war because it not only permitted an asymmetric and deadly war against the Japanese urban population, which was contrary to previous air force doctrine, but also prepared the way for the apotheosis of indiscriminate destruction in the two atomic attacks in August 1945. By inflicting massive damage on civilian urban areas through conventional incendiary bombing, the threshold of atomic bombing was easier to cross. In March 1945, Arnold hoped that LeMay would soon be able to "destroy entire industrial cities," something even the atomic bombs were not expected to achieve at one blow.[2] At the Potsdam Conference of the major Allies in July 1945, Arnold explained that thanks to the bombing, Japan was likely to surrender within three months as a nation "without cities."[3] The alteration of American air force strategy to what has been called "urbicide"— the killing of cities, whether by conventional or nuclear attack— remains a central factor in the unfolding air offensive in 1945.

The onset of incendiary bombing was far from a foregone conclusion. Once the islands had been captured in the Marianas, Arnold wanted a bombing campaign that still privileged precision targets, like the campaign in China. In preparation, a new bomber force, the Twenty-First Bomber Command, was activated at the Smoky Hill Army Air Field in Kansas on March 1, 1944. Arnold chose as its commander Brig. Gen. Haywood "Possum" Hansell (nicknamed because he allegedly looked like one), an Air Corps Tactical School instructor in the 1930s, a veteran officer of the Eighth Air Force in Europe, and chief of staff of the Twentieth Air Force. He took over the Twenty-First Bomber Command on August 28, 1944, to be succeeded as chief of staff in Washington by Norstad. It was planned that the new command would eventually have 1,000 B-29 bombers, but the initial force was less than 100, not least because the facilities, runways, and stores were far from complete when Hansell arrived in Saipan. The air forces depended almost entirely on the U.S. Navy to supply construction engineers and to ferry the supplies across the long logistic route from Sacramento in California to the new island bases. Hansell faced similar problems to those confronting LeMay in China. The runways and hard stands for the bombers were not complete, while much of the space was taken up by tactical aircraft, which were moved only after vigorous protest. The headquarters on Guam was not ready, and combat had not yet finished against the Japanese garrison on the island. The supplies sent to help construct the base were dumped in haste in the jungle and never recovered.[4] It was many months before the new bases were adequate for the task ahead; air crews and officers ate tinned rations and lived in army tents while the construction was completed.

Hansell was an enthusiast for the idea that selected industrial, transport, and utility targets, bombed precisely in formation from altitude by day, would fulfill Arnold's plan for the new bomber command to make an immediate and decisive impact. "One of the greatest factors in the defeat of Japan," Arnold wrote to Hansell in September 1944, "will be the air effort . . . every bomb that is added to each airplane that takes off for Japan will directly affect the length of the war."[5] Hansell established a program of intensive training for pilots who had expected nighttime bombing. Most had less than one hundred hours of flight time, far less in formation flying; there were too few operators for the new ground radar sets who had an adequate understanding of how to use the equipment; and the crews were expected to fly a round-trip of up to 3,000 miles over ocean with very little experience. There was also little good intelligence on Japanese targets. Photoreconnaissance was hampered almost continuously by cloud and industrial haze, and the first successful day of photographing occurred only on October 31 when the weather suddenly and briefly cleared. The Army Map Service employed geographers to supply target maps, who used among other sources the Japanese Imperial Land Survey, but until maps became available, finding industrial targets was intelligent guesswork.[6] The bases were also the object of Japanese air attacks. In November, eleven B-29s were destroyed, eight crippled, and thirty-five damaged.[7]

Pressed to show results, Hansell planned two raids against Tokyo, San Antonio I and II, to be carried out in the latter half of November. Strong doubts about the feasibility of the operation were expressed by other air force commanders. Even Arnold expressed reservations, despite his urgent need for results. The first operation, scheduled for November 17, 1944, had to be canceled because of high winds; the attack finally took place on November 24 when 111 B-29s, some flown by crews that had only arrived the week before, dropped 277 tons of bombs on the Nakajima aircraft plant and the Tokyo docks. Only forty-eight bombs hit the factory area, destroying 1 percent of the plant, and twenty-three of the aircraft failed to bomb because of fuel and mechanical problems. San Antonio II was carried out on November 27, but Tokyo was clouded over entirely, and bombs were dropped by radar, inflicting little damage. The greatest hazard was meteorological. At 30,000 feet over Japan, the jet stream reached up to 200 miles per hour, pushing the B-29s to more than 400 miles per hour, making accurate bombing almost impossible. Hansell lamented to Arnold that a combination of wind, weather, and poor visibility made the campaign difficult to mount. He was asked instead to try incendiary attacks,

also from high altitude, as an experiment. He did so on Tokyo
on November 29 using only twenty-nine aircraft and on Nagoya
on December 18, 1944, and January 3, 1945, but the results from
attacks mounted from 29,000–30,000 feet, in high winds, were
poor. The incendiary clusters were widely dispersed as they fell and
did little damage. Hansell told Arnold that he was "far from satis-
fied with the state of efficiency" that his force had demonstrated,
while the crews became progressively demoralized.[8] A report from
the air force doctors on Saipan, "Human Elements of the Operation of This Command," suggested that most crews just did their
mission without enthusiasm, hoping to survive in what was viewed
as a pointless campaign.[9]

Arnold almost certainly became disenchanted with Hansell's
leadership very quickly. There was little positive in Hansell's regular correspondence, but instead a litany of complaints about conditions and possibilities. The problems were real enough, as they had
been for the Eighth Air Force in England in 1942 as it struggled
to establish bases and a supply system, taking almost a year before
bombing a German target. Conditions were much worse on the
small Pacific islands from which the B-29s were intended to operate. The poor results led Arnold to stifle reports for the American
press to avoid unhelpful criticism. In mid-January, Norstad arrived
at Hansell's headquarters on Guam to tell him that he was to be
replaced by LeMay, who was to move from the China-India theater.
Hansell was surprised and disappointed and refused the offer to
serve under LeMay as vice commander. One of Hansell's colleagues
recalled Norstad's remark that perhaps Hansell was "too civilized
to fight the war the way it had to be fought," which now included
incendiary bombing. Hansell allegedly responded that "even if the
Japanese acted as beasts, Americans should not do the same. Killing innocent civilians was a matter of moral and ethical consideration" and was indeed contrary to the laws of war as United States

forces understood them.[10] In choosing LeMay, known to his crews as "Iron Ass," Arnold found the ideal commander for escalating the bombing war. Neither at the time nor in the postwar years did LeMay show any compunction about bombing and killing civilians if it helped to shorten the war.

LeMay still faced many of the same problems that had plagued his predecessor. The raids from mid-January to early March were made with more aircraft as numbers on the islands expanded and the maintenance system improved, but aircraft still found it difficult to cope with the jet stream and regular cloud cover, which affected bombing accuracy as radar operators and bombardiers struggled to find and hit the designated targets. Calculations showed that visual bombing of targets in Tokyo could be made on only four days in March, in Nagoya and Kobe, the other key industrial cities, on only three days, and from April onward even fewer.[11] Arnold still wanted precision bombing, if possible, but the eight raids on the Musashino aviation plant in Tokyo achieved very little. The persistent technical problems with the B-29 meant that in January, 21 percent of aircraft on average were not serviceable, while only 3 percent of the force had been lost to enemy action. Although the number of sorties flown increased by 18 percent between January and February 1945, the number of aircraft flown into Saipan had increased by 123 percent.[12] By early March, LeMay understood that current operations still failed to produce what Arnold wanted. He began to plan a radical change in tactics, flying low instead of high, flying at night, removing the bomber's guns to increase bomb tonnage, flying singly rather than in formation, and, above all, fully loaded with the new M-69 cluster of incendiaries, which were filled with jellied gasoline (better known now as napalm). LeMay famously claimed later that he carried out the subsequent fire raid on central Tokyo without telling Arnold. It was, he told the cowriter of his memoirs, "My decision and my order."[13]

The truth was more complicated. The prevailing view in the American air forces saw city bombing as neither morally nor strategically sensible. Ira Eaker, who later in 1945 was stationed in Washington as deputy commander of the Army Air Forces, wrote four years earlier that "bombing attacks on civil populace are uneconomical and unwise," a view that army commanders willingly endorsed. Although Arnold is on record in 1940 claiming that "Use of incendiaries against cities is contrary to our national policy of attacking only military objectives," he was nevertheless impressed during the war by the strategy of area bombing with incendiaries adopted by RAF Bomber Command in the course of 1941.[14] The two air forces collaborated closely on the technology and tactics of incendiary bombing. The British Air Ministry used the reports on incendiary bombing produced by the American Office of Scientific Research and Development; experts from the United States Fire Protection Service visited the British Research and Experiments Department (RE8) to give advice about how to start and sustain a major conflagration, and one of them stayed throughout the war. The two air forces experimented with different kinds of incendiary devices and shared the results.[15] By 1943, Arnold had developed his thinking about the strategic use of incendiaries by the American bomber force: to burn down industrial targets vulnerable to fire; to light a beacon by day in the densely populated areas of German cities for the RAF bombers arriving by night; or for burning down densely built-up areas "when the occasion warrants."[16] Although the Eighth Air Force was not formally directed to bomb "areas," bombers by 1944 routinely carried a 50 percent incendiary load on raids in which poor visibility made radar bombing, which was inherently less accurate, a necessity.[17]

Throughout the air war fought by the United States, incendiary bombing was the subject of regular planning, thinking, and technical development. In October 1942, the National Defense Research Committee produced a long report on the "Theory and Tactics of Incendiary Bombing" where the term "area bombing" was used for the first time. The report argued that in total war, even "the houses of workers are also prime objectives." Japanese cities, it was noted, are "especially good targets for incendiaries."[18] From early 1943, when Arnold asked the Committee of Operation Analysts to consider targets in Japan, they included in the provisional lists "industrial areas" because of the belief that Japanese war industry was decentralized into small supplier workshops embedded in residential zones and would be seriously affected by their loss. The advantages expected from incendiary bombing were widely canvassed. The Foreign Economic Administration authored a report in February 1943 on the disruptive economic effects from area attacks, which reflected the claims made by the British Air Ministry and Ministry of Economic Warfare that "de-housing" and the loss of amenities would lead to worker absenteeism, death, injury, evacuation, and the costs of rehabilitation.[19]

In May 1943, the United States air forces intelligence section asked for a report on the flammability of Japanese cities. The Office of Strategic Services (OSS) prepared maps of twenty cities, which were divided into zones that indicated the degree of vulnerability to fire. They included "Tokyo: Inflammable areas," which had already been drafted in November 1942.[20] The mapping formed the basis of the work of the Joint Target Group in Washington, which by February 1945 had developed an elaborate zoning system for urban targets, remarkably similar to the zoning pattern used by RAF Bomber Command from 1942 onward. Residential zone "R" was divided into R1 (fully built up), R2 (moderately built up), R3 (sparsely built up); the rest of the urban area included zones M for manufacturing, X for mixed residential-industrial, S for storage, and T for transportation. The priority zones were R1 and zone X, which contained the most congested housing. It was here that the initial fires started by the incendiary clusters would merge into a "tertiary fire" on a large and uncontrollable scale.[21]

To test the capacity of current incendiary bombs to destroy Japanese housing, models were made of "workers' quarters" at the Dugway Proving Ground in Utah, near Salt Lake City. British researchers set up similar buildings at a base near Watford, where typical Japanese houses were built alongside German. At Dugway, each Japanese house, made of a mix of Douglas fir and spruce wood, had two floors furnished in typical Japanese style with rice straw "tatami" mats, wooden screens, cushions, and sparse furniture. Tests carried out at Dugway between May and June 1943, in which the Japanese village was bombed twenty-seven times, demonstrated that enough "appliance fires" (i.e., those needing the fire service) could be started to justify incendiary bombing; by extension, it was calculated that seventy-five tons of incendiaries would be needed for each aiming point to start a fire that would run out of control. British bombs were generally less successful than the bomb now favored by the Army Air Forces, the M-69 incendiary, whose napalm filling was invented by a Harvard scientist, Louis Fieser, and demonstrated for the first time in July 1942.[22] Arnold seems not to have been aware of the Dugway tests and in February 1944 ordered a further investigation at Eglin Field in Florida, in an area where the climate most closely approximated Tokyo in the summer months. This was part of the Incendiary Evaluation Project conducted together with British experts by the Edgewood Arsenal, a secret facility on Chesapeake Bay in Maryland. Tests again confirmed the satisfactory vulnerability to fire of the standard Japanese home.[23] The testing showed that fires could best be started from an altitude of approximately 5,000 feet, the height eventually chosen by LeMay for the raid on Tokyo. In the case of the Japanese capital, studies confirmed that more than 90 percent of the city was composed of flammable structures.[24]

By 1944, both Arnold and the various committees charged with evaluating Japanese targets had reached the conclusion incrementally that incendiary bombing had the potential for inflicting critical damage on the chief Japanese cities. In August 1944, the Joint Incendiary Committee, set up by the Committee of Operation Analysts to work out how best to burn down Japanese cities, proffered the grim conclusion that firebombing of the six largest cities in Japan would destroy at least 70 percent of the urban area and reduce war production by at least 15 percent. On one of the few occasions when human casualties were candidly considered, the committee calculated that the bombing would cause the death of 560,000 by "suffocation, incineration, and heat."[25] Although Arnold and the Joint Chiefs of Staff were shown the report, it did not follow that the suggestion would be implemented, because priority was still given to destruction of the Japanese air force and aviation industry, but Arnold had long harbored the knowledge that enemy cities were a prime incendiary target. In February 1944, he told Roosevelt that with 1,700 tons of incendiaries, the air forces could cause uncontrollable conflagrations in twenty Japanese cities.[26] By February 1945, Arnold and his staff favored incendiary bombing if that would do more than the lame precision attacks so far undertaken.

LeMay must almost certainly have been aware of the drift in air force thinking, so that the Tokyo raid was not authorized in a vacuum. LeMay himself had undertaken an incendiary raid against the German city of Münster in October 1943 and later against the Chinese city of Hankou [Hankow] in December 1944 to disrupt Japanese traffic through the port. Postraid evidence showed that 60 percent of Hankou's central area had been destroyed by fire. By the time LeMay arrived in Guam, the Joint Target Group had produced a list of twenty-two cities suitable for area attack with incendi-aries. Like Hansell, LeMay was also pressured from Washington in February to extend the disappointing run of experimental incendi-ary attacks. On February 4, 1945, he conducted a high-level incendi-ary raid on Kobe with a modest 154 tons of M-69 clusters and again on February 10 against the Nakajima aircraft plant at Ōta, in which twelve bombers were lost and twenty-nine damaged out of a force of eighty-four aircraft. Finally, on February 24, Tokyo was raided by 192 B-29s carrying 454 tons of incendiaries.[27] This time significant damage was done despite the operational difficulties. Around 10 per-cent of the urban area was burnt out. By the time LeMay decided on the radical step of massive low-level firebombing, the incendiary option was already developed as a plan, favored by the command-ers in Washington, and understood to promise innovative levels of damage. "My reasoning," wrote LeMay in his memoirs, "told me I was heading toward a correct decision," but it was a decision shaped by the context in which the bombing of Japan was now discussed.[28]

THERE WAS NEVERTHELESS NO formal directive to LeMay to undertake on the night of March 9–10, 1945, a raid that he code-named Operation MEETINGHOUSE. The directive sent to the Twenty-First Bomber Command on February 19 did not specify an incendiary campaign against civilian areas, unlike the famous direc-tive to RAF Bomber Command on February 14, 1942, to attack as the sole priority the "morale of the enemy civilian population," with a list attached of German cities to bomb.[29] LeMay prepared the raid against a background of complaints from the crews, who now had to fly at night, without the protection of guns, and at low level, when their intensive training over the previous weeks had been on high-level bombing by day. When he addressed the crews before the operation, one of his officers objected that the plan looked like "the kind of terror bombing used by the RAF that our air force has been trying to avoid." LeMay allegedly replied "you simply can't fight a war without civilian casualties" and continued the briefing.[30] Air intelligence had prepared a mission description for the crews that justified the raid in economic terms as an attack on war workers in which "Employment at scores of war plants . . . would be directly affected."[31] The pilots were told to concentrate the bombing, marked by the lead aircraft with bright flares and the large M-47 gel bomb, on the most crowded wards of the city where the population density was more than 100,000 per square mile—Honjo ward and Fuka-gawa ward to the east, as far as the Johban rail track to the north, and the Eitaibashi bridge to the south.[32] They had to fly in singly to avoid accidents, at around 5,000–7,000 feet, but to do so in quick succession so that the fire would rapidly build beyond the control of the civil defenders and the fire service.

It proved to be an unequal battle. Japanese air and antiaircraft defenses were poor by the standards achieved in the European war. LeMay gambled that flying low at night would surprise the enemy sufficiently to provide his crews with some immunity. As a result of regular attrition by American naval aircraft flying from carriers off the coast, the air defense of Tokyo numbered little more than one hundred aircraft of the Tenth Air Division under Lt. Gen. Kane-toshi Kondō on the night of March 9–10. The antiaircraft batteries were for either high-altitude interception or very low, but there was little antiaircraft fire for the height at which the B-29s were to attack. For the Japanese air defenses, the problem was the vast size of the wartime empire. American air intelligence calculated that on January 1, 1945, there were 883 heavy antiaircraft guns defending targets in China and Southeast Asia but only 405 defending the whole of Kyūshū and Honshū; the figures for searchlight batteries were 211 in mainland Asia, only 142 for the home islands.[33] As in the earlier fire-raising of Hamburg in July 1943, the bombers were helped by the meteorological conditions on the day—clear, dry, and with a strong wind of about twenty-eight miles per hour.

The Japanese authorities in Tokyo were nevertheless not unprepared for the American air offensive. In November 1943, the government announced the "Imperial Capital Important Zone Evacuation Plan" to create open spaces and zones to prevent the spread of fire. People housed near rail lines, major roads, munitions factories, and railway stations were required to move, and their houses were demolished.[34] A "B-29 Countermeasures Committee" knew a great deal about the bomber and its capabilities, although too little was done for active measures to counteract what the bomber might achieve.[35] Civil defense preparations were once again generally poor by European standards. There were few air-raid shelters, and people were expected to undertake responsibility for saving their own houses from fire. Civil defense was organized on a neighborhood basis, with everyone expected to take part. Each household was told to use water-soaked mats and household water stores to douse the fires and to use brooms and ladders to reach and remove incendiaries, after first dousing all the lights. The popular slogan "Air Raid! Water! Gas Mask! Switch" drilled into householders bore no relation to the reality of a raid by heavy bombers, which Japan had never experienced.[36] The fire service was antiquated, relying on limited water resources. Postwar evaluation of Tokyo fire protection found that water resources for fighting fire totalled eight gallons per person, whereas in a typical city in the United States the figure was 200–300 gallons. Fire drill was military in style but left firemen poorly trained for a major conflagration and civilians largely at the mercy of their own defense.[37]

The threat of bombing also prompted programs of evacuation from the major cities. A cabinet decision was taken on October 15, 1943, to initiate evacuation of children and adults who were inessential to the war effort. In December 1943, the first directive was issued as an "Outline for Carrying Out Urban Evacuation," but it was still effectively a voluntary decision.[38] In June 1944, a compulsory program for the evacuation of schoolchildren was announced, and by March 1945, 446,200 young Japanese were sent to the countryside or small towns with their teachers; a further 800,000 evacuated to relatives. With the onset of the firebombing, millions more left the cities, usually outside any government scheme and in some case in defiance of orders to stay put. The government also created its own evacuation problem by insisting on the demolition of 614,000 houses to make firebreaks and the forced displacement of 3.5 million people. By August 1945, there were more than 10 million evacuees, raising the rural population from 42 million to 52.3 million. The population of Tokyo after March 1945 declined from 6.8 million to just 2.8 million; the other major cities declined by up to two-thirds of the 1940 figure.[39] There were plans to evacuate the emperor and his family to a massive bunker complex built with Korean and Chinese forced labor, but the monarch chose instead to live in a shelter complex under the palace. For those who evacuated, conditions were mixed. They exacerbated problems of food supply in the countryside, while many evacuees were struggling to cope with the loss of all their possessions. Schoolchildren were expected to undertake agricultural or war work for long hours and with scant provisions, but they avoided the bombs.

Operation MEETINGHOUSE was launched during the day on March 9 from all three island bases—Guam, Tinian, and Saipan—led by Brig. Gen. Tom Powers. Of the 334 aircraft that took off, the largest number so far in the war against Japan, 279 reached Tokyo and dropped 1,665 tons of incendiaries on the marker fires set by the pathfinders. They dropped 8,519 incendiary clusters releasing 496,000 six-pound bombs. Very soon hundreds of small fires were started that rapidly grew out of control into a larger conflagration. The small wooden houses had no protection as fire spread from roof to roof, with no spaces or firewalls to slow the flames. Aided by a wind that soon picked up speed to around 55 miles per hour, roads and firebreaks proved useless to prevent the onrush of fire. Although often referred to as a firestorm, the fire was a characteristic conflagration, moving leeward in a pillar close to the ground, burning everything combustible in its path, more turbulent than a firestorm and generating more heat and flame and less smoke. In six hours, the conflagration had burned almost 100 percent of the area in its path, including the interiors of more solid commercial and public buildings, where the wooden floors, stairways, and shutters on the inside burned out from the intense heat.[40] The conflagration was so hot that the B-29s flying above were buffeted by the rising heat waves. For the many thousands of civilians caught in the sudden raid, the result was catastrophic. Crowds surged away from the fires, confronting policemen who tried without success to force them back to save their houses, as the regulations required.

In the intense heat, sparks filled the air, setting fire to people's clothing and hair until they became another combustible object. Women in flight with their babies strapped to their backs failed in time to see that the infants were burning to death. One young survivor, Tsukiyama Mihoro, sheltered with his father under a railway bridge, beating out the sparks that fell like a rain, watching others around them self-combust. "One by one," he recalled, "without sin and regardless of age or sex, they became nothing but blackened clumps of charcoal." In the buildings where people crowded, including the large Meijiza Theater in the central Chuo district, the occupants were steamed, braised, asphyxiated, and finally reduced to a thick layer of ash, the buckles, helmets, and odd fragments of bone the only evidence that the ashes had been human beings.[41] Many sought to escape the flames in the parks or in the river Sumida, which divided Tokyo, but the thousands pursued by the heat into the open spaces found the effort fruitless. The French journalist Robert Guillain later recounted the fate of the throng that crowded onto the bridges from Honjo and Asakusa wards: "The spans were made of steel that gradually heated; human clusters clinging to the white-hot railings finally let go, fell into the water and were carried off by the current . . . thousands of drowned bodies were later recovered from the estuary." In the morning, Guillain was told, the incinerated quarter of the city was filled with crowds piled together in grotesque charred heaps; the wind now scattered some of the bodies as gray dust.[42] A total of 267,000 buildings were destroyed and just over 1 million left homeless. Initial police estimates suggested about 83,000 had perished, although the completeness of the destruction of the bodies made a firm figure difficult to arrive at. The death toll will never be known exactly but it is almost certainly higher than the official figures. The memorial to the bomb victims in Tokyo counts 104,500 from all the raids on the city.[43]

None of the scene on the ground was visible to those doing the bombing. The commander, Tom Powers, who circled the city to watch his crews complete their bombing runs, later wrote that he watched "until the holocaust had spread into a seething, swirling ocean of fire, engulfing the city below for miles in every direction."[44] The B-29s were little affected by Japanese defenses, either antiaircraft fire or night-fighter interception. At his headquarters, LeMay remained tense throughout the night of the raid. "I'm sweating this one out," he told his public-relations officer, St. Clair McElway. "A lot could go wrong."[45] From LeMay's perspective, the results were more than he could have hoped for. Almost sixteen square miles of Tokyo was reduced to ash for the cost of fourteen B-29s (two to enemy action) and damage to forty-two more.[46] Once photoreconnaissance had confirmed the destruction, LeMay was free to publicize what had been achieved. The news was welcomed with enthusiasm by his commanders because it seemed at last that the claims of the air forces were no longer merely speculative. Arnold wrote to LeMay later in March that the raid was "brilliantly planned and executed."[47] Norstad wrote to LeMay in early April that thanks to the bombing, "the XXI Bomber Command, more than any other service or weapon, is in a position to do something decisive" to end the war.[48] LeMay replied that the raids presented the Army Air Forces for the first time "with the opportunity of proving the power of the strategic air arm. . . . I feel that the destruction of Japan's ability to wage war lies within the capability of this command."[49]

The public reaction was immediate. The *New York Times* headline on March 10 captured the mood: TREMENDOUS FIRES LEAP UP IN THICKLY POPULATED CENTER OF BIG CITY. This came only weeks after the press had responded critically to the bombing of Dresden on the night of February 14–15 when it was suggested by an officer at General Eisenhower's headquarters that civilians might have been a deliberate target (and 25,000 died in the firestorm). The *Boston Globe* reporter Martin Sheridan was on one of the B-29s and on March 10 reported that over Tokyo, he had "never seen such a display of destruction" on the waterfront areas, "the most densely populated section in the world."[50] On March 15, the Intelligence Report of the Twenty-First Bomber Command carried photographs of the burnt-out city: "Less than 15 per cent of the No. 1 incendiary zone remains standing. Beautiful!"[51] The Pentagon worried that the publicity on the devastation of heavily populated areas would give the impression that civilians were deliberately targeted, although civilian casualties seem not to have been discussed at all in the publicity after the raid. McElway was asked to tell newspaper correspondents that precision bombing had not been abandoned and to "guard against anyone stating that this is area bombing."[52]

The reporting in Japan was controlled by government censorship, but the *Photographic Weekly Report*, issued nationally by the Cabinet Information Office, carried images of the destruction in the first issue after the raid, on March 28. The enemy, ran the editorial, "has adopted the most barbarous, scorched-earth, geno-cidal tactic" for which Japan must find revenge. The public was instructed to evacuate the cities, but for Tokyo the object was to start planting staple crops on the burnt-out landscape to provide "victory's provisions."[33] The *Report* also carried a photograph of the Emperor Hirohito, in full military uniform, on a tour of the dev-astated capital on March 18. Hirohito drove in a limousine to the bombed area, but then chose to walk through the ruins, offering a rare glimpse for ordinary Japanese of their ruler. Little was reported of the visit, though the emperor observed that the destruction was even worse than the Great Kantō Earthquake of 1923. On the day of the raid itself, March 9, Hirohito told his confidant, Kido Kōichi, that means should be contemplated for "ways to end the war."[34]

THE TOKYO RAID WAS only the beginning of a campaign of massive urban destruction. In addition to the 15.8 square miles burnt out in Tokyo on March 9–10, a further 162 square miles was destroyed in 66 urban areas, killing according to official figures a total of 269,187 people in just over five months of raiding.[35] Of all these raids, the "Great Kantō Fire Raid," as the firebombing of Tokyo came to be called in Japan, was the most exceptional. The number who died in just three hours of bombing at the center of the Kantō Plain represented the largest number of civilians killed on any one day in all the wars of the twentieth century. Indeed, the dead numbered more than twice the total who died over the whole course of the nine-month Blitz on Britain and more than three times the number killed in the raid on Dresden, the deadliest of the raids in the European theater. Although Tokyo has been over-shadowed by the two atomic bombs in postwar memory and much of the postwar historical literature, this raid more than any other deserves an explanation to match the enormity of the event.

There is no simple explanation for the willingness of LeMay and his force—encouraged to try urban area bombing through the evolution of air force targeting plans—to destroy a heavily populated urban area and to continue to do so over the months that followed. The cause commonly cited has been the ambition of the Army Air Forces to make a decisive contribution to the defeat of Japan to match the effort made by the U.S. Army in Southeast Asia and the U.S. Navy across the Pacific, a contribution that might underpin efforts to establish an autonomous air arm after the war. From early in the B-29 campaign, Norstad and Arnold stressed how important results would be for the future of the air force and its postwar profile. In late September 1944, Norstad told LeMay that "the B-29 project has a tremendous significance on the future of the Air Forces"; in mid-December 1944, Arnold reinforced the point to LeMay that the B-29 "is important to me because I am convinced that it is vital to the future of the Army Air Forces."[56] Arnold's impatience with Hansell in late 1944 stemmed from the failure to destroy targets when he wanted the public to see destruction.[57] One of the reasons Arnold so liked the area bombing was the visual effect it would have on the American public, on politicians, and on the rival service chiefs. Measuring results by city area destroyed became the norm after Tokyo, making a mockery of the idea of precision bombing. At the Potsdam Conference, Arnold suggested that bombing alone might bring the war to an end by autumn 1945, and to underline his conviction, he brought with him booklets for distribution filled with maps of the destroyed urban areas.[58]

LeMay was conspicuous among those who thought the power of the bombers might bring Japanese defeat and by implication strengthen the air force case. When Arnold visited him at Guam on June 13, 1945, LeMay was confident enough to predict that by October 1, when his city hit-list would be complete, the war would be as good as over. When Arnold sent LeMay in his stead to a meeting with Truman on June 18, he recorded in his diary that the bombing campaign had to be unhindered and quick, "that means Navy and Army must keep hands off."[39] The place of the air offensive in helping the air force claim to independence continued to be debated in the postwar period when separate reports were produced to demonstrate the value of the contributions made by the Navy and Army Air Forces in defeating Japan and prompting surrender. Maj. Gen. Orvil Anderson, who had served as deputy director of operations for the Eighth Air Force in Europe and ran the Military Analysis Division after the war, wrote in "Air Campaigns of the Pacific War" that "Air Power dominated naval warfare. Air power dominated ground warfare. Air power was capable of forcing the capitulation of an enemy nation without surface invasion." His intention was to promote the idea of an independent air force, a conclusion already recommended in the postwar United States Strategic Bombing Survey.[60] The extent to which the bombing of Japan directly contributed to the creation of an independent air service under the terms of the National Security Act of 1947 is open to debate, but there is little doubt that this final political achievement was an ambition among those organizing the aerial offensive that took priority over any sensitivity as to its nature.

The second possible purpose behind the area bombing campaign was revenge against an enemy pilloried for its atrocious behavior and routinely denigrated, often in racist terms, by those carrying out the air campaigns. Revenge was not a factor formally acknowledged, nor was racial difference explicitly used to justify a strategy that was carried out by the United States air forces in Asia rather than in Europe. But in both cases, these were familiar sentiments, casually mobilized to justify what was being done. The common reference points in seeking revenge, or redress, were the assault on Pearl Harbor in December 1941 and the Bataan Death March in May 1942, when 80,000 American and Filipino prisoners were marched in columns across the Bataan Peninsula after American defeat on the Philippines. Thousands died or were murdered on the way. Outrage over the surprise attack on Pearl Harbor was a persistent trope in American views of the Japanese enemy, and it featured in LeMay's own account of why bombing cities seemed morally justified, even if wildly disproportionate. When details of the Bataan Death March were finally revealed to the public in 1944, American opinion was again outraged (though most of those who died were Filipino); this, too, featured in LeMay's view of why revenge was justified. For LeMay, there was no issue about whether killing 87,000 people in a single night, chiefly civilians, was questionable: "Enemy cities were pulverized and fried to a crisp. It was something they asked for and something they got." In his memoirs, he wrote without regret about the people "we scorched, and boiled and baked to death."[61]

The behavior of Japanese soldiers in the defense of Manila in spring 1945 helped to sustain the sense of revenge against an atrocious enemy. The commander of the air forces supporting Gen. Douglas MacArthur in the South Pacific, Gen. George Kenney, thought that the Japanese were a "low order of humanity," whose soldiers indulged their "Mongol liking for looting, arson, massacre and rape."[62] After visiting the Philippines in April 1945, Arnold worried little about the deaths of Japanese civilians. In June, visiting LeMay in Guam, he found that atrocity stories had created a positive desire to inflict suffering on the Japanese (or Japs, as Arnold routinely called them): "There is no feeling here of sparing any Japs, men, women, and children: gas, fire, anything to exterminate the entire race. . . . These are not pretty stories but they explain why the Japs can expect anything."[63] In the United States, revelations of Japanese atrocities fired up hatred for the enemy, already embedded in popular discourse. *Life* magazine in May 1945 claimed that hating the Germans was not natural to Americans, "but hating Japs comes natural—as natural as fighting Indians once was."

The *New York Times* claimed without foundation in June that at least 1 million Japanese had already died under the bombing, but the claim prompted no protest from a public now eager for news of Japanese deaths.[64] Even Truman could note in his diary on July 25 that "The Japs are savages, ruthless, merciless, and fanatic."[65] At home and at the front, the Japanese were collectively viewed in animalized terms—monkeys were the most prevalent, but also as vermin or insects to be eradicated one way or another.[66] The view of the Japanese among those fighting the war in the Pacific did not cause the firebombing, but it contributed to blunting any concern among both officers and men for inflicting mass death on civilians who were unwittingly made to represent a people tarred as savage and primitive.

The denigration and dehumanization of the Japanese people also created a psychological distance, to match the literal distance, between those inflicting the bombing and the victims below on the ground. The U.S. Army would never have entered Tokyo and slaughtered 87,000 people in cold blood, but bombing, both here and in the war in Europe, made it possible to see the areas below as targets on a map, defined in strategic terms, but not as human spaces filled with people. Mapping of selected urban zones, with specified aiming points, enhanced the sense that these were geographic rather than human targets, even for air crews who were told that the zones were heavily populated. The claim that urban bombing would destroy industry, communications, and densely packed buildings turned the zones on the map into abstract space.[67] This was a reality that the air forces were keen to maintain to avoid any accusation that the Americans were imitating RAF Bomber Command's obliteration bombing in Europe. A summary of B-29 Tactical Mission Reports from June 1945, sent to the British Air Ministry, defined the distinction: "It is noteworthy that the object of these [area] attacks was not to bomb indiscriminately civilian populations. The object <u>was</u> to destroy the <u>industrial and strategic targets</u> concentrated in the urban areas." Yet only a week before, the London Mission of the American Office of Scientific Research and Development had asked the Air Ministry for details of the "damage assessment of domestic areas" from British urban bombing, "since they are now interested in area raids."[68]

The effort not to define the firebombing as area bombing of civilians continued throughout the campaign. The justification, first developed by the Committee of Operation Analysts in 1943, was that Japanese war production, unlike German, was distributed throughout an urban network of small craft shops, often in private homes.[69] It was therefore difficult to destroy this production except by burning down whole areas with the homes and workers as well. By 1945, this claim had become widely accepted. An Air Intelligence Report produced for the Twenty-First Bomber Command in late March 1945, spelling out the argument for bombing so-called invisible industry, pointed to "the tremendous part played in war production by the small household industries, thousands of little shops often located in a front or back room of individual residences, or small 'factories' consisting of hardly more than a couple of lathes operated by a few people.... They can best be destroyed by widespread conflagrations."[70] That the firebombing was essentially about hitting military and military-economic targets became a mantra for those carrying it out, as it was for RAF Bomber Command when bombing urban areas in Europe. "These raids," claimed LeMay in a speech in November 1945, "were not conceived as terror raids against the civilian population of Japan. But we had to be realistic."[71] When Secretary of War Henry Stimson worried that there had been a change of strategy in targeting whole cities, he was assured by Arnold in June 1945, according to his diary, that although every effort was being made to keep casualties down as far as possible, Japanese production units were "scattered out and were

small and closely connected in site with the houses of their employ-
ees," and therefore impossible to hit without danger to civilians.[72]

Arnold continued to define the area bombing of cities as if they
were in some sense precise targets, consistent with the regular effort
to carry out precision bombing of industrial targets by day, which
masked what was being done at night. LeMay's public-relations officer found a useful term for the area bombing that linked the two
kinds of raids together. In an article in the *New York Times* in June,
he suggested that the Twenty-First Bomber Command undertook
"pin-point incendiary bombing from a low level."[73] When Norstad
was asked directly if there had been a switch in air force strategy,
he simply replied "none." Norstad was even able to argue to Carl
Spaatz, overall commander of strategic air forces in the Pacific from
July 1945, that reservations he and others had expressed about the
use of the atomic bomb could be challenged by "the accuracy with
which the bomb was placed." Pinpoint nuclear bombing, continued
Norstad, ought to allay any anxiety that the project involved "wanton, indiscriminate bombing."[74]

AMERICAN AIR FORCE AMBITION, the demonization of the
Japanese enemy, and the effort to define area targets as legitimate
military-economic ones all ensured that the incendiary campaign
once begun would not be reversed. After the major raid on Tokyo,
LeMay immediately began plans to attack the other major cities
identified earlier by the Committee of Operation Analysts. Two
days after Tokyo, Nagoya was raided, but this time with much less
operational success. LeMay had chosen to send in bombers in waves
separated by an hour, which gave the fire service enough time to
control any major conflagration. Only 2.05 square miles burned
down.[75] On March 13–14, Osaka was bombed with concentrated
incendiary clusters, and eight square miles of the city was burned

out for the loss of one aircraft. On March 17–18, Kobe was attacked by 370 B-29s carrying 2,355 tons of incendiaries, considerably more than the Tokyo raid, burning down 20 percent of the urban area. One night later, Nagoya was bombed again, this time in a concentrated pattern, and a further three square miles was burned out.[76] On the four further raids in March, the winds were light, preventing the kind of conflagration that devastated Tokyo. Casualties were also low by comparison, as evacuation had rapidly taken place after the Tokyo raid: 3,988 dead in Osaka, 2,669 in Kobe. In contrast to all earlier raids of the Twenty-First Bomber Command, 92 percent of aircraft found the primary target, against a previous figure of 58 percent. Because the primary target was now the center of a major city, the improvement was not difficult to explain. Because of the change in tactics, it was also possible for the B-29s, flying at lower altitudes, to carry an average of 6.8 tons of bombs compared with 3.1 tons at high altitude. To LeMay's frustration, having found what he regarded as the most efficient way to use his force, the supply of incendiary bombs dried up. The need for a large tonnage of incendiaries had not been anticipated, and the U.S. Navy, preparing for the major invasion of Okinawa in April, had little incentive to deliver supplies for the air force. More bombs arrived by April 19, but these ran out by the middle of May.

LeMay now found his force compelled to transfer to other targets. The Joint Chiefs of Staff instructed the Twenty-First Bomber Command to raid Japanese air bases on the island of Kyūshū to suppress attacks on the fleet and on the amphibious forces attacking Okinawa. LeMay later complained it was "Target Nothing," because Japanese aircraft were mostly concealed.[77] The command was also ordered to take part in the mining campaign around the coast and major ports to contribute to the naval blockade. Over the following weeks, bombers dropped 12,135 mines, accounting, according to the postwar Strategic Bombing Survey, for 770,000 tons of destroyed or disabled shipping and 478,000 tons damaged.[78] When the incendiary stockpile increased in May, LeMay was allowed to continue with the firebombing. His force attacked Tokyo twice on May 23–24 and 25–26 with a total of 9,000 tons of incendiaries, burning out another nineteen square miles of the capital, including much of the imperial palace, forcing Hirohito to spend the rest of the war in the palace bunker. In June, once further bombs arrived, the fire-raising campaign intensified, with 22,000 tons of incendiaries dropped on fifteen targets.[79]

By this time, the Joint Target Group had fully adopted the incendiary campaign—it could identify no particular industrial bottleneck in the Japanese war economy for precision attacks—and listed thirty-three area targets for LeMay to demolish.[80] Like Harris in the RAF Bomber Command campaign in Europe, who kept a list of German cities to be crossed off each time he considered one "devastated," LeMay had a list of up to sixty cities that his force attacked systematically from June to mid-August, including many that were small and short of obvious military targets. The bombers flew more sorties and dropped a greater tonnage of bombs on fifty-two small cities than on the larger ones, in nine cases erasing more than 75 percent of the urban area, in six cases more than 70 percent. Japanese sources later listed bombing and shelling damage of some kind to 215 cities and towns.[81] Because of the decline of Japanese air opposition, due partly to the attrition imposed by American naval aircraft and partly because aircraft were kept back for the expected homeland invasion, more of the incendiary raids could be made by day. In June, 2,096 sorties by day dropped 12,000 tons, but 1,521 sorties by night dropped only 9,974 tons.[82] The Twenty-First Bomber Command now possessed an average of 791 serviceable bombers in June and 923 in July, giving LeMay a force capable of massive devastation. Arnold told the Joint Chiefs of Staff in July that LeMay's force could now "make possible the complete destruction of interior Japan," perhaps even compel Japanese capitulation.[83] This was an apocalyptic threat from a chief of staff who had earlier wanted only precision attacks. It illustrates well how the claims of wartime necessity could radicalize operational choices.

The incendiary campaign was complemented by the survival of more precise bombing of industrial targets. Seeking to avoid the problems of his early command when targets were attacked from 30,000 feet, LeMay ordered operations against specific industrial targets to be carried out at medium height and using incendiaries as well as high-explosive bombs. The "Empire Plan" for destruction of the Japanese air industry began in June 1945 and continued into July, absorbing 22 percent of the bombing effort. Oil was added as a target, though oil refineries were now in many cases no longer functioning because supplies from the southern empire had been cut off by naval blockade. Raids against the aluminum industry also hit plants with little capacity to produce because of raw material shortages. After the Urgent Dispersal of Plants Act in February, the Japanese authorities ordered dispersal of key plants once the major air offensive began the following month. Major companies began to move into smaller towns, using schools, breweries, and department stores as replacement capacity, or moved into caves and tunnels. By the end of the war, only around 20 percent of the dispersal program had been completed, but in many cases a relocated plant became by chance the victim of LeMay's campaign against smaller urban areas. Dispersal highlighted the problems faced by the transport industry, which had been ordered in the spring to give priority to food shipments, and the difficulty of keeping together a workforce from cities already bombed. Resources and labor for new construction were difficult to find. The cumulative effect of bombing, decentralization, and a lack of basic materials meant that the aircraft industry, the largest war industry in Japan, utilized only 50 percent of its capacity by the end of June 1945.[84]

At the point where United States bombing was fast running

out of targets to destroy, the RAF began to press the case for a British contribution to the campaign. The proposal was first mooted in late 1943, following the first Quebec Conference, but the condition for the British chiefs of staff was the defeat of Germany first, when resources would at last be freed from the European bombing campaign for transfer to the Pacific. Roosevelt was keen for British participation to signal to the American public that the British would pull their weight in the defeat of Japan.[85] When the British suggested participation, the American joint chiefs in June 1944 gave provisional acceptance for an RAF campaign beginning tentatively in mid-1945, but in October they insisted that nothing could be planned until bases nearer to Japan were captured. The first site the British were offered was northern Luzon, in the Philippines, well out of range of the Japanese home islands; by April 1945, the offer had moved to one of the Ryūkyū Islands still to be captured, Miyako Jima.[86] The American chiefs expected the British to furnish the engineering workers to construct the air bases but did agree to supply much of the equipment. The British Joint Planning Staff suggested a force of twenty heavy-bomber squadrons (both the Avro Lancaster, mainstay of RAF Bomber Command against Germany, and the Avro Lincoln, a derivative of the Lancaster with longer range and larger bomb load) to be operational against Japan between January and March 1946. By May 1945, the obvious difficulties in transferring aircraft, men, and equipment, together with the reluctance of the Canadian government to honor the initial plan to send a large contingent of its own bombers, scaled down the program to eleven squadrons of what was now called "Tiger Force," commanded by Air Vice Marshal Hugh Lloyd. The assumption was that the British bombers would help "to soften up Japan" by nighttime incendiary attacks, but the American side asked for the British to deploy the large blast bombs used at the end of the war in Europe—"Tallboy" and "Grand Slam"—because by the time the RAF arrived, there would be little left to burn down.[87] This chimed with a report produced by the British scientist Jacob Bronowski for the Air Ministry, which argued that blast bombs would be just as effective a way of destroying any remaining Japanese targets, reversing the strategy pursued by RAF Bomber Command against Germany.[88]

With hindsight, it is difficult to understand why the RAF wanted to participate given the logistic difficulties and the modest level of commitment. Political reasoning seems to have been significant, since Britain wanted a role in defeating Japan apart from the inconclusive campaigns in Southeast Asia. The Pacific war was for all intents and purposes an American one, but the absence of the British Empire at the kill would indicate clearly the relative decline of British power compared with American. It might also incite public hostility in the United States, wrote the British ambassador in Washington, Lord Halifax, which would be "in the highest degree unfortunate for us."[89] In June 1945, Churchill wrote to the Canadian prime minister, McKenzie King, that "it is of future importance to us all that a British Commonwealth force should participate in the strategic bombing of Japan" but without specifying why.[90] A few weeks earlier, the RAF chief of staff, Air Chief Marshal Charles Portal, wrote to Arnold's deputy, Ira Eaker, that it was "most necessary on the highest grounds of policy—from your point of view no less than from ours—that we take our part." Portal added that the British were keen to get at the Japanese "in their home country," a reflection of how distant the Anglo-Japanese war in Burma was from any prospect of inflicting defeat on Japan.[91]

The view of the American services was generally unsympathetic. The U.S. Navy did not want to collaborate with the British, though eventually a small Royal Navy Pacific Fleet did take part in the last weeks of the war. Nimitz tried to obstruct the provision of bases on Okinawa to the RAF. Arnold was hostile to the idea that the British might try to claim some of the credit for air force victory, if it came, while it was essential to find space for more B-29 groups and the arrival of the Eighth Air Force from Europe, intended for Okinawa as well. Lloyd was made aware of American resentment when he arrived in the Philippines in June. MacArthur informed him that "Arnold did not want the RAF to bomb Japan, and that he had obstructed our deployment to the best of his limited ability."[92] Churchill sent to Marshall his regret that the small contribution to the campaign was "nothing like what we should like to give you," and Marshall indeed regarded the small British contingent on offer as "an embarrassment."[93] The British, with reluctant agreement from the Americans, sent the first contingent of workers and supplies to build the Ryūkyū bases in June and July, but the plan eventually to base twenty squadrons of Lancasters and Lincolns by December 1946 were overtaken by events, and the bombing of Japan remained in American hands.[94] The British had the last word. In a report produced in 1946 on the bombing, the British Mission to Japan concluded that with such a feeble economy as Japan's, "no system of raids appears exceptionally intelligent or heroic."[95]

IN JULY 1945, the Joint Chiefs of Staff changed the command structure in the Pacific. Carl Spaatz became overall commander of the strategic air forces, LeMay became his chief of staff, and the Twentieth Air Force was taken over by Lt. Gen. Nathan Twining, another veteran of the war in Europe. The incendiary and precision bombing were maintained to the last and beyond. Because intensive bombing remained a formal strategic aim, there was no requirement to suspend it. During the period when the two atomic bombs were dropped, the Twentieth bombed a further eight targets, including a final flourish against Tokyo on August 14. The last raid of the war was made on the night of August 14–15 on an

oil facility at Akita, after the news that Emperor Hirohito was prepared to accept Allied terms.

A careful record was kept of the operations of the bomber
force over the summer of 1945. By the end of the war, the Twentieth Air Force bomber commands had attacked sixty-six urban
areas in a total of eighty-three raids, destroying 176 square miles
of urban area, some 40 percent of the targeted cities. Precision
attacks using principally high-explosive bombs numbered ninety-
one against fifty-six industrial targets, almost two-thirds against
thirty-one plants of the aircraft industry; testament to the problems in achieving accuracy with precision bombing, only thirty-
three of the missions were judged to have been successful.[96] In all
the bombing missions by the Twentieth and Twenty-First Bomber
Commands, 2,822 crewmembers were killed or missing in action
and 493 aircraft lost; in training in the United States, a further 461
died with the loss to accident of 272 aircraft.[97] What overall effect
the bombing operations had could not be known at the time and
could only be speculated on. Not until the United States Strategic Bombing Survey (Pacific Theater), under the direction of the
banker and wartime officeholder Paul Nitze, produced detailed
reports in 1946 of every aspect of the Japanese economy and society
under the bombs was it possible to arrive at a firmer judgment. In
June 1945, Arnold had met with the director of the United States
Strategic Bombing Survey (European Theater), Francis D'Olier, to
be briefed on the preliminary results. The European reports were
critical of incendiary bombing, chiefly practiced by RAF Bomber
Command, and found that it contributed relatively little to the
eventual decline of German war production. On the other hand,
attacks on oil and transport were regarded as critical, two target
systems that had not been recommended as a priority for Japan.
Arnold claimed to welcome the conclusions but did nothing to
alter the priorities of the offensive against Japan, where by August

1945 there had been just one dedicated mission against a transport target.[98] A new directive to attack sixty-seven transport targets was prepared only on August 11, too late to come into effect, though Spaatz confided to his diary that day his view that the plan was more likely to prompt surrender than the atomic bombs.[99]

When the United States Strategic Bombing Survey issued its main report on the Pacific theater in July 1946, its conclusions were mixed. It was impossible not to acknowledge that much of the crisis facing the Japanese war economy in 1945 was the product of the two-year naval blockade that cut Japan off from key supplies of raw materials and oil. Commodity imports into Japan were 20 million tons in 1941, 10.1 million tons in 1944, and a mere 2.7 million tons in 1945, by which time most of the trade consisted of vital food imports from mainland Asia. The supply of bauxite, essential for the aircraft industry, Japan's largest, was reduced from 900,000 tons in 1943 to a mere trickle of 15,000 tons in 1945; coking coal imports for the steel industry declined from 6.3 million tons in 1942 to just over half a million tons in 1945; and so on.[100] The index of Japanese munitions output (1941 = 100) reached a peak in September 1944 at 332 but was 156 by July 1945 partly due to bombing, but also because of the drying up of supplies and the program of industrial dispersal. Separating out the effects of air and navy proved a difficult task. The one clear conclusion was that incendiary and precision attacks did, according to the final report on the bombing campaign in September 1946, destroy or seriously damage twenty-five aircraft industry installations, thirteen oil storage and refinery sites, six major arsenals, and six other industrial plants. This was a thin list, even from an industrial economy as limited as that of Japan.

The urban area raids, on the other hand, were said to have destroyed 550 industrial installations, most of them small in scale, to match the wartime strategy supported by the target planners and by LeMay.[101] Although the Overall Report of the survey claimed that most home industry had been all but eliminated by 1944, small factories and workshops employing fewer than 250 workers supplied a high percentage of component parts and assemblies for the major plants, 50 percent in the case of Tokyo. Smaller manufacturing subcontractors did proliferate under the impact of war, though these were not home workshops. The number of manufacturing businesses expanded from 29,204 in 1940 to 48,307 by 1945. It was these medium-sized and smaller factories that were hit by the urban area campaign alongside the lives and homes of those who worked in them.[102] To that extent, the claim that burning down urban areas would contribute to inhibiting war production was not wholly wrong, even if it could not be statistically demonstrated with any precision. The Committee of Operation Analysts, however, concluded from the postwar research that it had been misleading to suggest area attacks against urban zones, which the committee had assumed during the war were filled with home workshops. The British Mission sent to Japan to report on the bombing suggested that the idea of home industry was a propaganda front by the Americans to show that raids on city residential areas had an industrial significance, "which American critics had denied to similar raids [by the RAF] in Europe."[103]

The postwar Strategic Bombing Survey also spent time assessing the impact of the bombing on the morale of the home population and unsurprisingly found that 64 percent of the large cohort interviewed claimed to have reached a point where they felt unable to go on with the war by 1945, the largest number because of the air raids.[104] The area attacks did indeed prompt a further deterioration in conditions on the Japanese home front, already affected by food shortages, long working hours, and the regimentation required by the state. The mass evacuation from the main cities, which reached panic proportions after the first major raid on Tokyo, disrupted the labor force, placed millions at the mercy of small towns and villages for shelter and food, neither of which the state supplied, and created a growing disenchantment with the war effort and the elite that spread contagiously through the areas where the evacuees arrived. Almost all those Japanese officials and officers interviewed after the war confirmed that the relentless incendiary bombing created a degree of social dislocation that, as Hayashi Keizo, the governor of Tottori Prefecture, put it, "reduced morale to zero."[105]

The Twentieth Air Force was used by the Psychological Warfare Branch, which operated from MacArthur's headquarters under Brig. Gen. Bonner Fellers, to exploit the social crisis with a pamphlet campaign not only warning about cities to be attacked but also prompting the population to leave, so that further confusion would be added to the problems generated by mass evacuation. The leaflets also encouraged the population to demand an end to the war by petitioning the emperor, or even to overthrow the warlords who had forced the people to fight, in the belief that bombing must provoke a social revolutionary reaction. This campaign, with more than 6 million leaflets and pamphlets, had as little effect as the effort in Europe by the British Political Warfare Executive to encourage the German people to revolt or suffer further bombing, and it reflected the degree to which American psychological warriors little understood the nature of the society they confronted.[106] The Special Higher Police, like the Gestapo in Germany, were alive to what they saw as the risk of widespread dissent as impoverished, hungry, resentful evacuees spilled out of the cities spreading rumors and antiwar sentiment. The Japanese political elite were preoccupied with fear of social upheaval. But there was no possibility of organized dissent in a heavily policed state, and indeed for the victims of the urban "de-housing" the priority was to survive, not to foment crisis. Bombing almost certainly left the affected population demoralized and aware of imminent defeat, but it did not sponsor a revolutionary wave.

There was no way in the summer of 1945 to demonstrate the impact of bombing on popular sentiment or on the development of the war economy. Both Arnold and LeMay believed that within months, Japan's war effort would be faced with collapse, LeMay by October at the latest, Arnold by November or December. The Joint Chiefs of Staff were unconvinced. Even with the sea-air blockade and intensive bombing, the Joint Intelligence Committee concluded that Japan might not surrender until late 1946, and despite Arnold's confidence that air power would deliver what was wanted within months, air force planning, both American and British, was predicated on a campaign that would indeed go on into 1946, perhaps 1947.[107] Arnold was asked by the joint chiefs for an answer to the question "Can Air Power alone defeat Japan?" The answer was discussed at a special meeting called by Roosevelt's successor, Harry S. Truman, on June 18, 1945, to discuss the future strategy for the Pacific. Arnold was supposed to attend the meeting but stayed in the Pacific. LeMay was sent instead and gave a briefing on the possibility that the bombing could finish Japan by October without an invasion. Marshall allegedly dozed through the presentation. LeMay concluded he had made no impact.

Marshall was firmly against the idea that an invasion of the Japanese home islands should be abandoned. According to the minutes, he added that "air power alone was not sufficient to put the Japanese out of the war." In an interview after the war, Marshall recalled: "We had killed 100,000 Japanese in one raid in one night, but it didn't mean a thing insofar as actually beating the Japanese."[108] The joint chiefs had already decided in late May that invasion was an unavoidable strategy. Marshall ordered planning for Operation "Downfall," a two-stage plan involving invasion of Kyūshū (Operation "Olympic") first by November 1945, and a second invasion of the plain around Tokyo (Operation "Coronet"), provisionally tabled for March 1946. The directive for "Olympic" was issued on June 20,

two days after the meeting. The Field Order for the forces involved
was issued later, on July 28.[109] Truman accepted the decision for invasion, worried that a siege strategy of bombing and blockade would
take too long.

Extensive though the destruction and social dislocation was as
a result of the bombing campaign, it did not prompt Japanese surrender any more than the bombing of Germany had done in the
European war, as Marshall understood. In Japan's case, Arnold's
view that defeat would arrive at a future date as Japan was destroyed
from end to end was not implausible, even if it cannot be demonstrated. The very negative impact of the bombing on Emperor Hirohito and the elite around him was evident well before the atomic
bombs (and will be explored more fully in chapter 4). The focus of
historical interest has nevertheless been on the two atomic attacks
where the link with surrender seems more clear-cut. It is worth
recalling that these two strikes were still bombing raids carried out
by the Twenty-First Bomber Command as part of the wider campaign from the air against Japanese cities. From the point of view of
the air force, Japan did not need to be invaded because air power,
old and new, ended the war.

CHAPTER 3

Why the Atomic Bombs?

At Los Alamos, we worked frantically so that a weapon
would be ready at the earliest moment. Once caught up in
such a mass effort, one did not debate at every moment,
in Hamlet fashion, its moral basis. . . . Every faculty, every
thought, every effort was directed to making that a success.

—ROBERT WILSON, LOS ALAMOS SCIENTIST, 1971[1]

THE ATOMIC ATTACKS ON HIROSHIMA AND NAGASAKI
were made possible chiefly by the willingness of the scientists
working at the Los Alamos laboratory complex, as Robert Wilson
later recalled, to devote every moment they could to making sure that
a bomb would be produced in time to be used during the war. The
production of the two bombs over a two-year period is a factor often
taken for granted, an illustration of the remarkable technical power
of the United States, but it was not inevitable that they would work
or that they would be produced to schedule. J. Robert Oppenheimer,

the Berkeley physicist and impresario of the laboratory, later claimed that he was "frantic to have the job done."[2] By May 1945, the scientists and engineers were working up to eighteen hours a day. "We had a goal," recalled one technician. "That's to make this thing as fast as possible, to make it work."[3]

Were it not for the maximum scientific effort by a cohort of the world's most distinguished physicists, the bomb would not have been ready by August 1945. There were many points when it seemed that the challenge to the engineers constructing the bomb or producing the fissile material it needed might not be met. There was nothing foreordained about the timing of when a bomb would be ready. When British scientists reported to the government in July 1941 that production of a bomb was a possibility, the earliest date suggested was late 1943. Among leading British scientists, including Friedrich Lindemann, Churchill's personal scientific adviser, there was strong doubt that this schedule could be met or that Britain possessed the resources to produce it.[4] In the United States, there was more optimism that it might be possible, and Roosevelt was anxious, as he told a meeting in October 1941, even before the United States was at war, that if a bomb could be made, America must not lose the race to make it. But there was skepticism here too, rightly as it turned out, that a bomb would be made in time to be used against Germany, although the Third Reich surrendered only three months before the first bomb was used. Yet Germany was the main priority. "If they [the Germans] succeeded first," claimed Arthur Compton, a key figure in the American nuclear program, "they would have in their hands the control of the world."[5] It was this possibility that goaded the initial scientific effort. As it became clearer just how long it would take to produce the fissile material—both uranium-235 (U235) and plutonium, a new element derived from uranium—the focus began to shift from use against Germany, whose defeat was expected in late 1944, to possible use against

Japan, whose defeat still seemed unpredictable. From spring 1943, a Military Policy Committee set up by the U.S. War Department to discuss the role of any possible bomb began to give preference to use in the Pacific, not Europe. At a reception celebrating the success of dropping a bomb on Japan, Oppenheimer expressed his one regret that the bomb had not been ready to drop on Hitler's Third Reich.[6]

THE STORY OF THE development of the bomb is by now well known and does not need repeating here in full. The breakthroughs achieved in nuclear physics by the end of the 1930s made the possibility of producing a nuclear weapon a real one. In the United States, the research began in 1939 with a $6,000 grant to the University of Chicago under the auspices of a Uranium Committee set up at Roosevelt's instigation. In Britain, following a report by two émigré German scientists, Otto Frisch and Rudolf Peierls, that a "super-bomb" could be made, a handful of leading theoretical physicists came together in an informal "U-Bomb Committee" ("U" for uranium), which began meeting in April 1940.[7] A few weeks later, the name was changed to the MAUD Committee to disguise its purpose, and it was the positive report from this committee, produced almost a year later, that accelerated the search for a viable weapon in Britain. The report was given to leading American scientists to show that a bomb could be produced, a conclusion that American nuclear researchers had already reached. In September 1941, the head of the National Defense Research Committee, James Conant, and the Berkeley nuclear physicist Ernest Lawrence met at the home of Arthur Compton, professor of physics at Chicago, to agree to proceed with an American project. On October 9, Vannevar Bush, director of Roosevelt's Office of Scientific Research and Development (OSRD), met the president to advise him that the research should be made urgent. The Uranium Committee was wound up, and in December 1941 a new section, coded S-1, was established under the OSRD with presidential authority to produce a bomb.[8] Compton co-opted scientists from across the country to work on the project in what was called the Metallurgical Laboratory, and it was here, a year later, that the first chain reaction was created in a disused Chicago sports facility by the Italian émigré physicist Enrico Fermi.

There soon opened a wide difference in the way the two Allied leaders responded to the prospect of a bomb produced by nuclear fission. Roosevelt grasped its significance almost at once. A month before S-1 was established, and two days after the meeting in October, Roosevelt asked Bush to draft a letter to Churchill suggesting that the two countries should pool their efforts or even jointly conduct a nuclear bomb program. Churchill failed to respond for weeks, and by the time he did so, with little apparent understanding of what had been offered, the American scientists had decided that it was better to proceed on their own.[9] At the same time, the MAUD Committee was wound up and the whole nuclear project handed over to Imperial Chemical Industries under the cover name "Tube Alloys." Any sense of urgency declined. Overall responsibility for the British nuclear bomb program was vested in the hands of a senior civil servant and lord president of the council, Sir John Anderson, while ICI ran the research program. The decision was relayed to the British chiefs of staff, who were enthusiastic, but Churchill minuted that he was "quite content with the existing explosives," though he would not stand "in the path of improvement." Even later, when more was known about the potential of a nuclear explosion, he could tell the Danish physicist Neils Bohr that "this new bomb is just going to be bigger than our present bombs"—an indication of how little he understood what a nuclear bomb implied.[10]

Roosevelt, on the other hand, with his country now at war,

wanted a project that could produce a bomb as quickly as scientif- ically possible, on the unspoken assumption that it could be used against the United States' new enemies. He financed the research project from a secret fund he controlled. Unlike Churchill, he was briefed in 1941 about the devastating scope of a nuclear explosion and so had no illusions about what was being produced. In June 1942, the S-1 group reported that a bomb could be made in reasonable time and, if successful, "will [not might] win the war."[11] Roosevelt directed that the project now be given over to the U.S. Army to cre- ate the industrial installations and bomb-producing facility to give substance to what had been largely theory. Churchill visited Roos- evelt the same month and allegedly drew from the president a prom- ise of collaboration, though the details were never written down, and by then the American scientists involved had created something of an iron curtain between themselves and fellow scientists in Britain and Canada. A year later during the first Quebec Conference, on August 19, 1943, Churchill and Roosevelt again discussed collabo- ration, and this time an agreement was drafted. Tube Alloys was to be wound up and several hundred British scientists were to join the American project; Roosevelt agreed that the consent of both Allies was needed for the use of a nuclear weapon; and a vague commit- ment was made to exchange information, which the American side deliberately sidestepped. The agreement did little to reverse the slide toward an almost completely American program of research and production on a scale that Britain could not have imitated, even had Churchill pursued nuclear weapons with his usual vigor.

Even if Roosevelt supported the nuclear option more firmly and consistently than Churchill, the success of the United States' proj- ect depended on two people appointed in 1942 to oversee the pro- duction of the fissile material and the bomb that would carry it. It was chance that produced them, as neither was a first choice. When Roosevelt agreed with Bush in June 1942 that the military should take over the bomb project to impose the necessary discipline and to procure the needed resources, the first director appointed from the U.S. Army Corps of Engineers was Col. James Marshall, who set up office in New York in what was now called the Manhattan Engineer District. He proved to be too slow to develop the project with the urgency needed, and in September, Secretary of War Henry Stimson decided on a change. He chose the man who had directed the construction of the new Pentagon building, Col. Leslie Groves, whose reputation for tough management preceded him. Groves had already been working for Marshall, so that when he was told his task was to produce a bomb by the earliest possible date "so as to bring the war to a conclusion," he already knew much of what was needed.[12] He was appointed on September 17 and set about his new task at once the following day, negotiating to buy a stockpile of uranium held by a Belgian mine company now based in New York. A day later he went to Tennessee to buy a site now called Oak Ridge, where a vast plant was constructed to carry out the separation of uranium isotope U235. Once it was understood that the plant could not at the same time cope with plutonium extraction, a new plant and workers' city was constructed at Hanford in Washington State by the DuPont Corporation, where plutonium would be extracted from the fissile material produced in a reactor. Groves's immediate energizing of what was now called the Manhattan Project made a remarkable difference to the possibility that a bomb could be produced during the span of the war.

The second appointment proved just as decisive. The S-1 Committee had been convinced of the viability of a bomb project by Oppenheimer, a young nuclear physicist at Berkeley who had been invited in spring 1942 to chair a group to consider how a bomb might be made. Oppenheimer is generally regarded as a mercurial character, ambitious, arrogant, sensitive, cultured, and anxious to make some kind of contribution to the United States as it faced the prospect of war. "I think if I were asked to do a job I could do really well and that needed doing," he wrote in spring 1941, "I'd not refuse."[13] Although one of the scientists involved in the theoretical discussions in late 1941 and early 1942, he had no formally defined role beyond chairing the group on how to make a possible bomb. Groves preferred as first choice the Berkeley physicist Ernest Lawrence, but he was too closely involved in the nuclear project in his home laboratory.[14] Oppenheimer's opportunity came when he met Groves in October and accompanied him on a long train journey. He believed that the only prospect for creating a bomb was to have a central laboratory in which a large cohort of scientists and engineers would work together, thinking, arguing, and finding solutions as a unit. Groves liked the idea and recruited Oppenheimer to create a laboratory out of thin air.

To find an appropriate site, the two men traveled to Oppenheimer's favorite area of the United States—the arid, mountainous core of New Mexico. On a high desert plateau, thirty-five miles from the city of Santa Fe, they found the Los Alamos Ranch School. The owners willingly sold their business, and the school became the center of what in a matter of months was a shantytown and laboratory complex of 45,000 acres, which eventually housed 4,000 civilian scientists and technicians and 2,000 soldiers. Los Alamos was entirely cut off from the outside world. When they arrived in Santa Fe, the scientists were directed to a solid seventeenth-century Spanish adobe house at 109 East Palace Avenue, the cover office for Los Alamos, to check in before they set off on the thirty-five-mile journey to the mesa, 7,000 feet above sea level. All letters out were censored before being mailed in Santa Fe, while letters in had to be collected from PO Box 1539 in the same town.[15] Accommodation was basic by the standards many of the scientists were used to. The OSRD insisted that none of them would receive additional pay for working in a remote and inhospitable location, cut off from their familiar surroundings.[16] In this complex, code-named Project Y, the bomb was designed and eventually built.

Oppenheimer's appointment as director of Los Alamos seems to have no clear date. His choice as scientific supremo was also at first not a certainty. The FBI had a thick file on his alleged contact with and activity for the American Communist Party, which would almost certainly have made void any attempt at security clearance. He also had no administrative experience of any kind, and was, in the absence of a Nobel Prize, regarded as a scientist of second rank compared with the many Nobel laureates recruited to the Manhattan Project. Groves and Oppenheimer were an odd couple—one all military bark and bite, the other a sensitive and caustic intellectual—but the synergy between them worked. In July 1943, by which time Oppenheimer had been running the complex for three months, Groves insisted that he be given security clearance so that his work could continue. Oppenheimer dropped all contact with communists he had known in California and insisted on his patriotic credentials. This did not prevent his security clearance from being revoked ten years later after a U.S. Senate hearing—the Gray Board—judged his reliability to be questionable.[17]

The science community created at Los Alamos was a unique one, and its willing contribution to the creation of an atomic bomb was decisive. The scientists were a select cohort, working at the very vanguard of the physics and chemistry necessary to make a bomb work. The lonely and beautiful mesa setting chosen by Oppenheimer, overshadowed by high peaks, within sight of the Rio Grande, helped to create a sense that here was a residual stretch of the romantic American frontier to match the challenging scientific frontier the scientists were now exploring. "Funny how the mountains always inspire our work," Oppenheimer told the reporter Lansing Lamont.[18] The scientists walked and talked across the landscape surrounding the complex, where the practical problems they faced could be thrashed out in the rich natural environment they now inhabited. That their work was of outstanding originality and purpose they seem to have had no doubt. "Never before," wrote Victor Weisskopf about his experience at the site, "had my colleagues or I lived through a period of so much learning, of so many insights into the structure of matter in all its manifestations." Their sense of wonder drove them on to see whether the theoretical breakthroughs, only a few years old, could be transformed into an engineered bomb.[19] That intense curiosity and uncertainty in almost all cases overcame any reservations about building as soon as possible a military tool of awesome destructive power.

Overseeing the whole project was Oppenheimer, with regular prompts from Groves and his military team. Despite the uncertainty in Washington about both his loyalty and his competence, those working for him found him to be a remarkably effective executive. Two of his colleagues later defended his reputation against accusations of questionable leadership. He was, wrote Hans Bethe and Robert Christy, "a brilliant leader of Los Alamos.... He was aware of both the latest successes and the most important unresolved questions. And he kept us all informed."[20] The regular sharing of information between the different divisions working at the laboratory, against Groves's preference for compartmentalization, gave the project a democratic character, essential to the rapid solution of problems, and may well represent Oppenheimer's most important contribution. Each of the scientists on arrival was presented with the "Los Alamos Primer," which set out the science involved and the nature of the proposed bomb, including the prognosis that neutron radiation would affect life within 1,000 yards of the bomb, and that the blast would destroy an area two miles from ground zero. In mid-April 1943, Oppenheimer organized a major conference of all involved to identify what needed to be done.[21] Information was thereafter shared by a small governing board, a larger coordinating

council of approximately sixty people, and finally a regular collo-
quium of up to 300 scientists, where progress and problems were
discussed and solutions proposed.[22] When British scientists began
to arrive in 1944—some of them German refugees, including Otto
Frisch and Klaus Fuchs, the Soviet spy—Groves wanted them cor-
ralled in their own section, but Oppenheimer distributed them to
the different departments on the basis of their specialism. Their
contribution, Groves later insisted, had been "helpful but not vital,"
but this ignored the experience British scientists had had in calculating blast effects from the bombing war in Europe.[23]

The scientists worked in the knowledge that an adequate supply
of the fissile material would not be available until 1945, so that the
main task was to solve the engineering problems for two distinct
bomb types—a bomb using uranium-235 and a bomb using pluto-
nium-239. The first employed a "gun" mechanism, shooting a unit
of the uranium material into a fissile core to begin a chain reaction.
When the same design was proposed for the plutonium bomb, it
was discovered that the material would fission spontaneously, producing a premature explosion at a lower level of yield. The discovery
provoked a temporary crisis in spring 1944 over the feasibility of
the bomb, until Seth Neddermeyer and one of the Tube Alloy scientists now attached to Project Y, James Tuck, proposed a solution.
The plutonium would be surrounded by a casing of charges whose
explosive impact would implode the plutonium, setting off the necessary chain reaction at the right moment.[24] The implosion bomb
and the "gun"-design bomb were both developed over the year that
followed, the uranium bomb nicknamed Little Boy, the plutonium
bomb, which was now a very large construction, called "Fat Man"
rather than the original "Thin Man." The scientists involved in
the implosion version had great difficulty in designing the charges
that surrounded the core, and the final bomb design was not completed until February 1945. Oppenheimer selected what he called a

"Cowpuncher Committee" to "ride herd" on the final months of "Fat Man" development to keep it on time. At one point, the leader of the division responsible had to use a dentist's drill all night to remove the small air pockets that persisted in the cast material of the charges. So uncertain was the result that Groves had to be persuaded later, against his better judgment, to allow a test of the plutonium bomb to ensure that the science worked.[25]

As the program developed and the promised fissile material seemed likely to become available, the pace and urgency of work at Los Alamos increased. In October 1944, a factory siren was introduced to bring the scientists to work and to end their working day. In August 1944, Capt. William Parsons, an ordnance expert, became associate director of the complex, responsible for speeding up the development of an actual weapon that would be used eventually by the Army Air Forces. In November, he headed an Intermediate Scheduling Conference to impose a strict regime of coordination and timekeeping on the different research divisions, but the evidence from those who worked on the bomb suggests that the scientists needed little prompting to work long hours and collaborate on problem solving. Bethe and Christy recalled that the scientists "felt that we were part of the lab and that each of us was personally responsible for its success."[26] It was in this sense that completing the project successfully, as Robert Wilson recalled, became an inescapable obligation for those involved, setting aside any concerns about how the bomb might be used.

That it would be used if completed in time was implicit in the program scheduling. In what circumstances it would be employed was a different question. In 1943, one section of Los Alamos was already involved in calculating the effect of the bomb on different targets. A naval base or a harbor was explored as a possibility, but neither air blast nor underwater explosion was expected to achieve enough, and Oppenheimer insisted in December 1943 that the idea should be abandoned. Oppenheimer and Parsons both favored a city, where the blast effects would be greatest for a bomb dropped from 30,000 feet. They dismissed the idea of a demonstration explosion to show the enemy what to expect, which a proportion of scientists working on the Manhattan Project preferred. Oppenheimer wrote to Groves in October 1944 about the "fallacy of regarding a controlled test as the culmination of the work of this laboratory."[27] A city, German or Japanese, was the preference of those who led the nuclear program. Not until the late autumn of 1944 did it become clear that bombs would be ready the following year. In December, Groves informed Roosevelt that a uranium bomb would be ready by August 1, 1945, and a plutonium bomb, once it had been tested, soon after. Roosevelt told his secretary, "If it works, and pray God it does, it will save many American lives."[28]

In April 1945, a second Target Committee was established composed of representatives from the Army Air Forces and Los Alamos, paralleling the Target Committee for the incendiary bombing. By the time of its first meeting on April 27, Truman had been informed about the bomb project. Roosevelt had told his vice president nothing about it, but at Truman's swearing in as president, the future secretary of state, James Byrnes, told him that Stimson would explain to him a bomb that might be capable of "wiping out entire cities and killing people on an unprecedented scale." On April 25, Stimson confirmed to the new president that "one bomb could destroy an entire city," leaving Truman, like his predecessor, with no illusions about the damage an atomic bomb could do.[29] Truman was not involved in the discussion of the target that followed his initiation into the project secret. The Target Committee met in Oppenheimer's office at Los Alamos on May 9–10, 1945, to discuss all the aspects of a bomb attack from the height of detonation to the coordination necessary with the program of the Twenty-First Bomber Command. The committee agreed that the target should be an urban area at least three miles wide, susceptible to massive blast effect, and not yet destroyed by incendiary bombing. The air force had been asked to avoid the area bombing of five targets: Kyoto, Hiroshima, Yokohama, Kokura, and Niigata. The atomic bomb operation was supposed to achieve spectacular psychological effects, though the meeting did not conclude that it would end the war. Discussion finished with the suggestion that the Twenty-First Bomber Command might follow up with an incendiary attack the following day to create a "serious conflagration," evidence that the two forms of attack were seen as complementary.[30] At the final meeting of the Target Committee on May 28, the decision was taken to recommend placing the first bomb "in center of selected city" where scientists could observe more clearly the technical capabilities of the weapon. The industrial zones were regarded as too dispersed and distant from the center to justify placing a bomb there.[31]

By this time, the operational planning for the use of the bomb was nearing completion. On May 30, the British scientist James Chadwick, discoverer of the neutron and head of the Tube Alloys mission to the United States, sent to Churchill and Sir John Anderson the "Outline Plan for Employment of Special Weapon." The target priorities were Kyoto, Hiroshima, and Niigata, to be bombed from 30,000 feet with bombs that would burst above ground. The first bomb, the uranium "Little Boy," was planned to be operational from August 1, the second, the plutonium "Fat Man," a week later. There would be a delay before the next uranium bombs were ready, the second by November 20, the third by December 24. Three "Fat Men" were expected each month. Hiroshima and Niigata were thought to need two bombs each, Kyoto at least four; the complete destruction of the targets was expected only by December 1945 if the war lasted that long.[32]

The planning for the atomic raids was considered a military responsibility, but in late May, Stimson decided to create yet another body, the Interim Committee, including the leading scientists who had first authorized a nuclear program, to advise Truman on the wider implications of the proposed bombing. After much debate, the meeting of the new committee on May 31 followed the Target Committee in recommending early use against Japan on a target city with military industry surrounded by workers' housing and without prior warning, but concluded that selection of the target was "essentially a military decision," as it was. Stimson, who chaired the group, wanted to be sure "the objective was military damage . . . not civilian lives," but the final conclusion made civilians an obvious target, despite his reservations.[33] To confirm the technical possibilities, a Scientific Panel from Los Alamos joined the discussion; Oppenheimer speculated that 20,000 dead would be one result. The panel convened again at Los Alamos on June 16 to consider the operational conclusions, and Oppenheimer once again led the argument against a demonstration. The meeting concluded that "we see no acceptable alternative to direct military use."[34] For those who built the bomb, there was an irresistible scientific curiosity about whether it would work and with what results. A prevailing sentiment, according to one of the British party at Los Alamos, was "fear of failure."[35]

Just as there were reservations over the incendiary bombing of Japanese cities, the stark realization that a nuclear bomb was a reality and was to be used for military purposes prompted a minor revolt among some of the scientists working on the Manhattan Project away from Los Alamos. The bomb was not a central concern for them as it was for Oppenheimer and his large team at the site in New Mexico. When Enrico Fermi visited from Chicago, he was impressed by the pace and resolution at Los Alamos: "I believe you people really *want* to make a bomb."[36] Compton's Metallurgical Laboratory at the University of Chicago housed most of those who were reluctant to accept military use of what was essentially the fruit of their own research. Groves chafed over scientists "of doubtful discretion and uncertain loyalty," but their influence was limited. Under the leadership of James Franck, a report was produced and sent to Stimson on June 12 recommending a demonstration explosion on an island or in a desert to show the Japanese what to expect, but only to use the bomb in anger if the demonstration failed to bring an end to hostilities. In July, Compton polled 150 scientists and found 69 in favor of a test run; a second poll found 72 percent of the MetLab staff in favor of a demonstration and only 15 percent in favor of immediate military use.[37] The main driver of the protest, Leo Szilard—a key player in the early plans for the nuclear program—organized a petition against military use and went to Washington to deliver it in person to Truman, only to be denied access and to be told by Byrnes, now Truman's secretary of state, that the bomb would be used.[38] The petition reached Stimson, who seemed to be as anxious over the use of the bomb against civilian targets as he was over the targeting of city populations in the incendiary campaign. He insisted, against the strong objections of Groves, on removing Kyoto as the priority target for reasons that have been much debated. The popular view that he had a sentimental attraction for the city following a visit decades before is supported by little solid evidence. He did understand that the city was a key symbol of ancient Japan and that its destruction might be regarded as a particularly wanton act by a people about to be defeated and occupied.[39] He also reiterated his concern at the meeting of the Interim Committee at the end of May that "we could not concentrate on a civilian area," and that meant Kyoto. By mid-June the target list was Hiroshima, Niigata, and Kokura; Nagasaki was added in July. Stimson, despite his anxieties, made no real effort to prevent an atomic bomb from being dropped on the cities that remained on the list, any more than he had tried to prevent LeMay's firebombing campaign once it had started.

The arguments surrounding the targeting and its ethical implications hinged still on the capacity of the scientists to show that a fission bomb worked. After the scientists at Los Alamos had persuaded Groves that a test of the more complex plutonium bomb was an essential prelude to dropping the "gadget"—the euphemism used for "Fat Man"—on a live target, the test became a benchmark for the whole project. As a result, the pressure on those involved with engineering the bomb reached an intense pitch the closer the possibility of success approached. In March, the scientists and the army found a site some 230 miles southwest of Los Alamos, on the Alamogordo Bombing Range (renamed the White Sands Proving Ground shortly before the test). The site was a bleak stretch of arid land overlooked by distant mountains. There were a few ranch buildings, supplemented by rushed and primitive accommodation that at first housed 160 civilian and military personnel; by June, a further 210 scientists and technicians arrived to supervise the installation of the test equipment and to install the test bomb.[40] The test, given the code name Trinity by Oppenheimer, added a new range of technical and practical problems. The adobe tracks could not cope with the heavy traffic, and Groves reluctantly agreed to construct at very short notice twenty-five miles of tarmac roads. Nearby air force trainees twice bombed the site in error, mistaking the lighted area for their assigned target. Miles of cable had to be buried to avoid damage, but communication across the zone provided regular crises. In the two months before the scheduled date, the hundreds of technicians, engineers, and scientists struggled to solve problems that would otherwise have voided the test. When the test "Fat Man" was assembled at the top of the metal tower where it was to explode, it was found that the plutonium core would not fit the casing, causing a temporary panic. The core had expanded with the heat as it was driven to the site, and exposure to cold air reduced it down to the right size ensuring at almost the last moment that the test could go ahead.[41]

Authorities in Washington wanted the test conducted before Truman went to the Potsdam Conference, scheduled for mid-July, adding political pressure to the technical. For Truman and Gen. George Marshall, the bomb was not yet a proven certainty, but a successful test would add a new dimension to discussions with the other Allies about concluding the war with Japan. That the two bombs should eventually be used if a test worked had already been recommended by the Target Committee, the Interim Committee, and the Scientific Panel at Los Alamos, requiring only the approval of the military leadership and the president. The Joint Chiefs of Staff never debated the use of the bomb, so that the opposition on moral grounds to the use of the bomb expressed by the chair of the committee, Adm. William Leahy, was confined to the margins; Marshall supported the development and employment of the bomb, and his voice in the summer of 1945 carried more weight with the president.[42]

Discussions of atomic strategy were nevertheless academic until the Trinity test showed what a bomb could do. There was widespread anxiety among those involved that something might go wrong. Groves confided to the British ambassador his fear that unless he could "use at least one bomb during the present war," he would be grilled by a congressional investigation on a waste of public money.[43] Oppenheimer worried that if the test proved a dud, "I'll never get my people up to pitch again."[44] The scientists traveled on yellow school buses to Base Camp, so many that some had to be located twenty miles from the test site in the Compagna Hills. Hans Bethe told colleagues before the test that "Human calculation indicates that the experiment must succeed. But will nature act in conformity with our calculations?" The head of the

Alamogordo site, Kenneth Bainbridge, imagined having to check the bomb for what went wrong—some loose soldering, a circuit affected by the rain that fell heavily before the test, a fatigued technician making a wrong connection. He checked that all the master switches were on, and at 05:29:45 on the morning of July 16, the bomb exploded exactly as the science had predicted.[45] The impact on those who were present has often been described. Oppenheimer, demonstrably stressed and chain smoking for the whole night, was a changed man. Isidor Rabi, one of the scientific advisers on the project, witnessed his return to Base Camp from the observation bunker: "I'll never forget the way he stepped out of the car . . . his walk was like *High Noon*. . . . He had done it.[46]

Some eyewitnesses expressed an ambivalence over the vast destructive power released by nuclear fission. Bainbridge in the end thought it "a foul and awesome display"; the journalist William Laurence imagined it to resemble "the grand finale of a mighty symphony of the elements," both "fascinating and terrifying, uplifting and crushing."[47] Others were relieved and exhilarated that the bomb worked after more than two years of scientific effort. At Los Alamos, there was wild celebration. "The place was a madhouse," recalled one witness, "they were so pleased with themselves. They had worked so hard, and they had done it." One of the scientists recruited from Princeton led a snake dance through the complex, to the accompaniment of bongo drums.[48] James Chadwick wrote back to London on the day of the test that witnessing it "was a wonderful, even fantastic experience." He, like many others, had been anxious about the uncertainties of the test, but a week later he recalled that "the awe-inspiring nature of the outcome quite overwhelmed me . . . the reality was shattering." It was, he concluded, a "vision from the Book of Revelation."[49] A week later, another of the British scientists, William Penney, held a seminar to report on the test and its results in which he made clear just what the effects would be on buildings and their inhabitants when a bomb was dropped. Measurements suggested that the blast was equivalent to 20,000 tons of TNT.

The news was sent to Truman and Churchill at the Potsdam Conference, first a brief text that the test was successful, then on July 18 a fuller report on the results from Groves that reached Stimson three days later. "For the first time in history," he wrote, "there was a nuclear explosion. <u>And what an explosion</u>." The test, he continued, "was successful beyond the most optimistic expectations." Those present at Alamogordo, he added, wanted a positive use of the bomb to bring the war "to a speedy conclusion."[30] Following the initial news, Stimson recorded that Truman seemed "tremendously pepped up by it." When the president was told in Potsdam five days later that a bomb would soon be ready, Stimson again found him "immensely pleased." Truman confided to his diary that the "Japs" were now certain to fold up "when Manhattan appears over their homeland." Churchill was so excited at the news that he broke security by telling his doctor, Lord Moran, the following morning that "it is to be used upon Japan, on cities, not on armies."[31] For the British government, the test exposed the issue of whether there should be British consent to the use of the bomb as Roosevelt and Churchill had agreed at Quebec in 1943. The British were not told about the Interim Committee, nor of its approval to use the bomb as soon as possible on Japan. The British military chiefs were in the dark about the Manhattan Project until Churchill was persuaded in January 1945 to allow them to be told, but only in the presence of his scientific adviser, Friedrich Lindemann, who doubted that the bomb would work. "What fools the Americans will look," he claimed in April 1945, "after spending so much money."[32] Anderson advised Churchill in early May to insist on the letter of the Quebec agreement and to establish machinery for reaching a joint decision, but after exploring the possibility of discussing the issue with Truman and then abandoning the idea, the Combined Policy Committee in Washington on July 4 minuted

Churchill's agreement for use against Japan as a formality. British consent was assumed rather than asked for, but for the British side there was little alternative and no real opposition.[53]

There now followed a flurry of activity between Potsdam and Washington over the authorization for use of the bomb. Although Truman later wrote to his sister that he had had to make the "terrible decision" to use the bomb, "but I made it," he was distorting the reality. There is no clear record that he gave a directive to use the bomb. On July 22, he and Stimson discussed the earlier decision not to include Kyoto on the list of possible targets on the presumption that the bomb would be used on one of the four targets forwarded to Potsdam from Washington on the following day—Hiroshima, Niigata, Kokura, and Nagasaki.[54] Stimson also met with Gen. Henry Arnold three times between July 22 and 24 to discuss "where, why, and what effects" could be expected from what Arnold called the "Super bomb." Arnold said that he would send Col. John Stone to Washington to see Groves and Carl Spaatz and secure their recommendation.[55] Stone replied to Arnold on July 24, listing the four targets and their military significance, confirming that Spaatz and Ira Eaker, Arnold's deputy in Washington, both concurred.[56] The same day, Groves wired Marshall and Stimson to receive their approval for a nuclear operation, and the following day Marshall endorsed what was a fait accompli. On July 24, Spaatz had already been issued with a formal directive from the War Department, as he had requested, authorizing him to order the "first special bomb" operation on the first day of good weather after August 3 against one of the four designated targets, and the following day Spaatz wired his approval of the directive.[57] If there was a "decision" to drop the bomb, it was a collective one, reinforced by news of the successful test, and by the prior approval of Stimson's Interim Committee. Rather than giving a presidential directive, Truman's approval more nearly resembled a rubber stamp.

NO ISSUE IN THE history of the United States war effort has occasioned (and still occasions) greater debate than the dropping of the atomic bombs, first on Hiroshima and then Nagasaki. The question asked is usually "was it necessary?"; the question, however, should really be "why was it thought to be necessary at the time?" It is the answer to this second question that might explain why the most lethal weapon of this and of any war was unleashed against cities crammed with civilians. The straightforward answer is that the bombs were dropped to force Japanese surrender, end the war quickly, and save American lives. This answer is not wrong, but like the explanation for the firebombing of Japanese cities, the historical reality was far more complex. There is little doubt that the priority for United States forces in the summer of 1945 was to end the war as soon as possible. The campaign on Okinawa, which began in April 1945 and ended in June after months of bloody engagement, was taken as evidence of just how costly it was going to be to invade the main Japanese home islands. Total casualties for the campaign, both combat and noncombat, reached 82,229, including 12,520 dead, among them the American commander, Gen. Simon Bolivar Buckner. The decision to invade was taken at the strategy conference with Truman on June 18, but the minutes record that the president "had hoped that there was a possibility of preventing an Okinawa from one end of Japan to the other."[58] Much hinged on the estimates that Truman was given of the level of casualties expected from invasion of Kyūshū and Honshū, which varied widely between journalistic guesses and the detailed statistics supplied by the army.

At the meeting on June 18, Marshall supplied figures (which he warned were not entirely reliable) of the campaigns from the Philippines, Iwo Jima, and Okinawa. Combat casualties on Okinawa were close to the figure for the first thirty days of the Normandy invasion, which amounted to 42,000 killed, wounded, and missing, though noncombat casualties from illness and accident were almost as large. Douglas MacArthur, asked to supply figures for his South Pacific campaigns, reported 13,742 Allied dead against 310,165 Japanese, a ratio of 22:1.[59] But much higher estimates had circulated from 1944 onward. The Joint Planning Staff in August had suggested a figure of 500,000 dead during an invasion of the home islands, and this became a regular reference point. Lauris Norstad told Curtis LeMay that if his fire-bombing campaign worked, it would save one-half million American lives. The Army Service Forces, responsible for removing casualties, estimated 720,000 dead and wounded up to December 1946 if the campaign lasted that long. The figure of 1 million casualties—killed, wounded, noncombat—was suggested by former president Herbert Hoover and became a widely employed statistic to show how high the cost of invasion would be. Even though MacArthur and the Joint War Plans Committee arrived at far more modest estimates (approximately 100,000 battle casualties for the invasion of Kyūshū and the Tokyo plain together), Truman later recalled in his memoirs and postwar interviews the idea of 1 million as a measure of what was saved by the bombing.[60] It is worth recalling that the defeat of Germany had already cost 1,047,115 casualties of all kinds, a figure likely to encourage efforts to reduce the casualty rate in the Pacific.

Saving American lives was also a priority for Marshall given the probable difficulty in mobilizing and training additional army recruits from summer 1945 without public protest. In a meeting on May 29, 1945, with Stimson and Assistant Secretary of War John McCloy, in which the use of the bomb in some form on Japan was acknowledged, Marshall also brought up the question of using poison gas to speed the defeat of island garrisons holed up in tunnels and caves, and then to overcome the expected fanatical resistance on the home islands. The option of using gas did not involve a legal issue for the United States (which had failed to ratify the Geneva Protocol of 1925 prohibiting use of chemical and biological weapons), but Marshall understood that it was a moral threshold to cross, like the firebombing of city centers, and it was not employed in the European war. The Military Operations Division reported in mid-June 1945 that use of gas would "materially shorten the war." The Chemical Warfare Service had already considered Japan as a possible target for retaliatory gas attack from the air, and by January 1945 there were more than 6 million pounds of stored persistent chemicals available (those that did not rapidly disperse once used) and 483,000 bombs for carrying them.[61] Operation "Sphinx" was authorized by the War Department in May 1945 to investigate the most effective gas for use in ground warfare against troops concealed in bunkers, caves, and tunnels. Tests were conducted on goats and rabbits, confirming that mustard gas—widely used in the First World War, and the major gas stored in the Pacific theater—was the most effective. The results were relayed to the Army General Staff on July 11, 1945, a few days before the Trinity test.[62]

Gas was never used. The tactical and logistic preparations for doing so were still limited by summer 1945, but the idea of the "mass employment of gas throughout Japan," already mooted in June, showed the extent to which the intense desire to shorten the war and save American lives by any means was already embedded in the thinking of the military leadership before the atomic bomb made recourse to gas redundant. The successful test demonstrated that there was a shortcut to victory over Japan without the need for invasion and its high cost in lives. At the Trinity site, Groves's deputy, Brig. Gen. Thomas Farrell, a few minutes after the explosion famously announced, "The war is over!" Groves replied that it would be "as soon as we drop one or two on Japan."[63] Even this claim was uncertain as Groves knew. Like the use of gas, there was some discussion in the summer of using nuclear weapons in a tactical role against Japanese forces defending Kyūshū as a further means of reducing American casualties. On July 30, Groves informed Marshall of the probable effects of a battlefield atomic bomb, paralyzing an area one mile in diameter, and seriously affecting enemy combat to a radius of five miles. He informed Marshall that there would be three or four bombs in September, four or five in October, and five in November. After the bombing of Nagasaki, Marshall, who was unhappy about using bombs on urban areas, considered the possibility of supporting Operation "Olympic" by dropping a tactical nuclear weapon on defending troops just before the beach invasion, and then one on rear areas to confuse Japanese resistance. This idea, too, was made redundant by the Japanese capitulation.[64]

The decision to use the bomb to save American lives was also connected with American reading of the Japanese enemy. As it became clearer that the Japanese Army and Navy were preparing a large-scale defense of Kyūshū, easily identified by Japanese military leaders as the next American target after Okinawa, the casualty projections needed regular updating. American signals intelligence used the Japanese Army communications, whose codes were broken in 1943, to prepare a full picture of Japanese preparations. By the time of Truman's meeting on June 18, intelligence reports showed around 300,000 Japanese troops on Kyūshū, coastal areas mined, and the population moved away from the potential invasion areas. Over the following six weeks, estimated troop numbers increased to 534,000, then 600,000, presenting a much more dangerous scenario than the picture in June. Truman may well not have been told these figures, but for Marshall and the army planners, the Japanese buildup meant ever higher American casualties.[65] There was also information on the total mobilization of the Japanese population to face the final battle for the homeland, which suggested that the fanatical resistance predicted might indeed materialize. "THERE ARE NO CIVILIANS IN JAPAN" claimed an intelligence officer of the Fifth Air Force after news of Japan's national mobilization law in June, confirming the erosion of any distinction between combatant and noncombatant already evident in the conventional bombing of city centers.[66] The English-language *Nippon Times* gave no indication of a willingness to surrender unconditionally. An editorial in early July looked forward to the time "when every Japanese subject is made fully aware that to die for the Emperor is to live," commending the *kamikaze* code of "certain death, certain kill."[67] The Japanese Army counted on 28 million "militia" when planning the final battle, recruited from the wider citizenry in a People's Volunteer Fighting Corps established in May and confirmed as an obligation on citizens in June 1945. A "People's Handbook of Combat Resistance" explained how anything could be used as a weapon: "hatchets, sickles, hooks, and cleavers. In karate assault smash the Yankee in the pit of his stomach, or kick him in the testicles."[68]

On the question of when or whether Japan might surrender, the Allied Combined Intelligence Committee noted in June 1945 that the "idea of foreign occupation of the Japanese homeland, foreign custody of the person of the emperor, and the loss of prestige entailed by acceptance of 'unconditional surrender' are most revolting to the Japanese."[69] There was much argument in Washington over whether the stark terms of unconditional surrender might be modified to make it easier for the enemy to accept, and in particular whether it should be made clear that the emperor would be allowed to remain on the throne, an argument that Stimson tried to impress on the president in July.[70] But interception of Japanese diplomatic traffic to the embassy in the Soviet Union suggested that the Japanese government was seeking Soviet arbitration and the possibility of a compromise peace. At Potsdam, Stalin chose to tell Truman and Churchill about the Japanese approaches to underline that unconditional surrender was unacceptable in Tokyo, perhaps to make sure that the Western powers were still committed to it and would not seek a separate peace.[71]

Truman already knew of the Japanese initiative and had privately noted "a telegram from Jap emperor asking for peace," which was not quite the case.[72] Intelligence intercepts of the correspondence between Tokyo and the ambassador in Moscow in fact revealed continued resistance to the idea of unconditional surrender.[73] Truman was persuaded by Byrnes that it would be better to issue a clear reiteration of the demand for unconditional surrender and the conditions involved so that there would be no doubt about Allied intentions.[74] This was also intended to still any criticism at home over the government's attitude to surrender. The result was the Potsdam Declaration published on July 26 and signed by the United States, Britain, and China (the Soviet Union was not yet at war with Japan) spelling out the obligations under unconditional surrender and promising "prompt and utter destruction" if the terms were not agreed. Truman was doubtful it would have the desired result, but the operational directive for the use of the atomic bombs had already been issued in the hope that the shock generated by the new weapon would prompt Japanese compliance. Even in this case, there remained doubt over whether a nuclear attack would produce the desired effect. Nevertheless, when the Japanese press reported two days later that the government would ignore the Potsdam Declaration (the word used, *mokusatsu*, has a number of possible meanings), there was no doubt that the bomb would now be used.[75]

The need to bring the war to a rapid end and perception of Japanese unwillingness to surrender are reasons enough to explain the outcome. But for many decades, beginning with the publication of Gar Alperovitz's *Atomic Diplomacy: Hiroshima and Potsdam* in 1965, at the height of the Cold War, the argument that geopolitical calculations, stemming from the awkward relationship with the Soviet Union, weighed more heavily on the decision-makers than concern over the costs of invasion has remained at the center of the debate over why the bombs were dropped.[76] On this argument, use of the bomb was a way of strengthening American bargaining

power over the future of Eastern Europe and East Asia and of lim-
iting Soviet ambitions, an early manifestation of the later strategy
of "containment." There is no argument that American politicians
were deeply concerned over Soviet behavior in Eastern Europe,
which had already demonstrated that Stalin's intention was to keep
the Western Allies at arm's length while consolidating Soviet security and political interests throughout the region. The American and
British reaction operated in something of a vacuum, because there
was no way of knowing what Kremlin leaders were thinking in the
absence of inside intelligence, while Stalin had ample information
on his allies, including detailed knowledge of the bomb, even the
date of the Trinity test and its results.[77] When Truman obliquely
informed Stalin on July 24 at Potsdam about a new weapon for use
against Japan, the Soviet dictator ordered the Soviet atomic research
program, already generously supplied with the fruits of Soviet espio-
nage, to be accelerated. After Hiroshima, the work was placed under
the supervision of the interior minister, Lavrenti Beria.

Stalin had begun to think seriously about Soviet strategy in
East Asia from autumn 1944, and his priority was to repeat what
was happening in Eastern Europe as the Red Army took control of
the conquered territories. He wanted guarantees of Soviet security
in both theaters of war. In December 1944, he made it known that
his aim was Soviet occupation of the Kurile Islands, the southern
half of Sakhalin Island, control over Outer Mongolia, a lease on the
ports of Darien (Dalian) and Port Arthur, and a controlling interest in the rail lines connecting the ports to the Soviet Union. These
aims were accepted at the Yalta Conference of February 4–11, 1945,
by Roosevelt and Churchill, who were keen to get Stalin to commit to war against Japan once Germany was defeated, but the effect
was to give to the Soviet Union carte blanche for the reordering
of East Asia at the expense not only of Japan but also of China.[78]
During the first months of 1945, Stalin turned to the issue of the

future of Korea and began to consider occupying the northern Japanese island of Hokkaido once Japan was defeated. At Yalta, a four-power occupation of Korea under United Nations trusteeship had been suggested, but Stalin knew that a Soviet invasion of Manchuria would carry the Red Army into Korea and with it perhaps the Korean communists in exile in Moscow as a putative government. In May 1945, Stalin told Harry Hopkins, Roosevelt's former confidant, that he hoped for zones of occupation in Japan, as in defeated Germany. By August, the Red Army in the east had been directed to develop operational planning for occupying Hokkaido after defeat of Japanese forces in Manchuria and Korea.[79] Soviet involvement in the war in Asia was more about securing postwar political gains than helping the United States defeat Japan.

American leaders in the summer of 1945 responded ambivalently to the promise of Soviet assistance in the war against Japan. On the one hand, as Marshall pointed out in the June 18 meeting, Soviet entry into the war "may well be the decisive action levering them into capitulation"; on the other hand, Byrnes and Stimson both thought it would be better to end the war without Soviet intervention. Stimson later recalled that "I felt it was of great importance to get the [Japanese] homeland into our hands before the Russians could put in any substantial claim to occupy and help rule it."[80] That ambivalence was evident at Potsdam. Truman was pleased to receive Stalin's confirmation that the Red Army would begin its invasion around August 15: "I've gotten what I came for," he wrote to his wife on July 18, "I'll say we'll end the war a year sooner now." But later the same day, after the initial report on the Trinity test, he wrote in his diary, "Believe Japs will fold up before Russia comes in."[81] A few days later, he asked Stimson whether the United States really did need Russian entry into the war, and on July 24 Stimson told the president that in Marshall's view, with the prospect of the bomb "we would not need the assistance of the Russians to conquer Japan."[82]

By this point, it would almost certainly have been impossible to prevent a Soviet invasion of Manchuria as Marshall and Truman both appreciated. Stalin now wanted the Soviet campaign accelerated initially to August 1, which the Soviet commander in the east, Marshal Aleksandr Vasilevskii, told him was not possible, then to August 11, and eventually, because of poor weather prospects on that date, to the early hours of August 9, when the invasion finally began. Stalin was evidently anxious in case Japan surrendered to the Americans before the Soviet Union had made the promised gains in the east. It is difficult to detect in these developments a deliberate strategy on the part of the United States' leaders at Potsdam to deploy the bomb for geopolitical motives in the hope of restraining Soviet ambitions in East Asia. Indeed, the effect of the bomb was the very opposite, accelerating Stalin's efforts to make substantial gains in Asia at American expense. As it became evident that the Red Army could occupy all of Korea, Marshall directed MacArthur to plan a speedy occupation of the peninsula under the code name "Blacklist II." Stalin eventually agreed to partition at the 38th Parallel, but not from fear of the bomb. He later told the Polish communist leader, Władysław Gomulka, that "not atomic bombs, but armies decide about war."[83] Certainly, the Soviet side interpreted the bomb as a potential threat. Andrei Gromyko later recalled Stalin's reaction: "They slay the Japanese and bully us. They want to force us to accept their plans ... on Europe and the world. Well, that's not going to happen."[84] The British embassy in Moscow later wrote to London that the Soviet press deplored the Anglo-American monopoly of the bomb as an attempt "to reduce the Soviet Union to a secondary role and change the balance of forces." In October 1945, the press further claimed that Western reactionaries who hoped to intimidate the Soviet Union with the bomb were "playing a dangerous game" by "intensifying Soviet suspicion of anti-Soviet tendency in capitalist countries."[85]

But for the United States, the priority was still to end the war and reduce its cost for the American people. In all the discussions about the use of the bomb in the months leading up to the test, military priorities prevailed. Defeat of Japan was what the American public and the armed forces in the Pacific wanted, and for Truman and Marshall the bomb was a possible though not a certain way of achieving that military goal. Intimidating the Soviet leadership may have been seen as a bonus, but it was not what the bomb had been produced for, nor why Marshall approved the military operation. By the summer there was anxiety among the U.S. Army leadership that the public would not support a prolonged campaign against Japan. Expectations of rapid demobilization after the defeat of Germany were disappointed. Japan was an obstacle, and any moral sensitivity about how defeat was to be achieved, already absent in popular enthusiasm for the conventional bombing campaign, had disappeared by the time of Potsdam. The *Chicago Tribune* ran a headline YOU CAN COOK THEM BETTER WITH GAS as popular support for gassing the Japanese increased from 23 percent in favor in a September 1943 poll to 40 percent in favor by June 1945.[86] One poll taken shortly after the atomic bombing showed 95 percent of respondents in favor; a Gallup poll on August 26 found 85 percent in favor; a further poll in the autumn showed that more than one-fifth of respondents wished that more had been dropped on Japan.[87]

A more significant factor in explaining the decision was the persistent pretense, maintained initially with the incendiary bombing campaign, that the target for the two atomic bombs would be military in character and therefore a legitimate one. This was achieved as with the incendiary raids by defining cities in terms of the industrial and military targets present rather than by the wide residential areas inhabited by civilian workers and their families. The Interim Committee approved use of the bomb "on a war plant surrounded by workers' homes."[88] Marshall was one of those keen to ensure that the bombs were to be used on "straight military objectives" as he told Stimson.[89] But the secretary of war was also anxious that the potential target should be more obviously military than was the case with the firebombing operations, which he regarded as morally dubious. The discussion of potential targets regularly emphasized their military significance in the hope of reducing the threat to civilians evident in conventional bombing. The military personnel and scientists involved in the bomb project were particularly interested in the blast effects of the bomb but, even though it was known about, paid little or no attention to the immediate radiation effects that involved people rather than buildings. The blast effects were initially uncertain—estimates ranged from the equivalent of 1,000 tons of TNT to 20,000 tons—and the measurements conducted at the Trinity test were designed to calculate the blast more accurately, as they did. In postwar investigation of the bomb sites in Japan, greater attention was paid to the consequences of the blast, while biological assessments of what happened to the human beings was of secondary significance. Groves tried in the weeks after the bombings to minimize the radiation effects as Japanese propaganda, and when evidence of mass deaths emerged, he told an investigating committee that doctors had assured him "it is a very pleasant way to die."[90]

In these calculations, human beings were largely absent, though not entirely unacknowledged. In a small handwritten note in his files, dated July 25, 1945, Arnold wrote a list of the agreed targets—Hiroshima, Kokura, Niigata, Nagasaki—with the estimated population next to each one, and a tick to indicate approval. Kyoto was also listed, population 155,200, but it appeared further down the paper, and with only a half tick, as though poised to acknowledge the agreement reached by Stimson and Truman that week not to include the ancient Japanese capital.[91] When Colonel Stone sent Arnold a list of the target cities a day earlier, he added their military character: "Hiroshima—'Army City,' embarkation, industry, 2 shipyards" and "Nagasaki—major shipping and industrial center."[92] It was at Potsdam in the final week of July that Truman asked Stimson to make sure that the target was going to be a military one: "I have told the Secretary of War, Mr. Stimson, to use it so that military objectives and soldiers and sailors are the target but not women and children." Truman added to his journal that he was reassured that the target would be "purely a military base."[93] The euphemism was sustained after the bomb was dropped on Hiroshima. In a radio address on August 10, Truman assured listeners that the first bomb was dropped on "purely a military base" because in the first attack "we did not want to destroy the lives of women and children and innocent civilians."[94] Historians are divided over whether this was deliberate self-deception or simply a lack of understanding about the impact of the bomb and the character of Hiroshima as a city, but the dominant theme throughout the bombing since March 1945 had been to sustain the image of a campaign not waged against civilians. It is difficult to understand how Truman any more than others involved in the decision to use the bomb could fail to grasp that thousands of civilians would perish, but it was a view consistent with the way in which Japanese cities had been represented in expediently abstract terms from the onset of the firebombing campaign. The tranquilizing effect of the military language used explains why Truman at the time had no reason to obstruct the bombing and every reason to endorse it.

THE CONDUCT OF THE operations against Hiroshima and Nagasaki was an entirely military affair despite the attention paid to the broader geostrategic context in much of what has been written about the bombs. The preparations had begun long before the Trinity test. In 1943, the idea of using a British bomber, the Avro Lancaster, to deliver the bomb had been briefly considered but rejected on account of its insufficient range and the hostility of the air force chief of staff, Henry Arnold. "There was no way," he later said, "they were going to deliver the American atomic bomb in a

British plane."[95] He favored the creation of a self-contained bombardment group. In September 1944, the 393rd Bombardment Squadron was chosen as the core of the 509th Composite Group, which was responsible for dropping the bombs. The crews commanded by Col. Paul Tibbets were based for training at Wendover Field, Utah, where they were supplied with dummy bombs and specially modified B-29 aircraft. In December they were posted to Cuba to practice long overseas flights. The group was destined for a high-security base on the island of Tinian, chosen in preference to Guam because it was one hundred miles closer to Japan. Work began in February 1945 with the same sense of urgency that drove preparations at Los Alamos. The personnel began to arrive in April, now directly under LeMay's command. All the details of the missions were discussed between LeMay and Groves in June, when LeMay was in Washington for the June 18 meeting.[96] The crews on Tinian trained with bombs modeled on "Fat Man," which carried 5,500 pounds of explosive and a proximity fuse to allow the bomb to burst in the air, as the atomic bombs were to do. They were nicknamed "Pumpkins" and used as cover for the real bombs by pretending they had a genuine tactical purpose. The facilities at the base were built over the summer, modeled it was said on the street layout of Manhattan; there were six 2-mile-long runways. A technical group from Los Alamos was sent to check the components as they arrived and to supervise the assembly of the bombs. This was still the point at which the missions might have been postponed. A B-29 carrying components suffered engine failure, while the USS *Indianapolis* was torpedoed and sunk by a Japanese submarine just after delivering a cargo of bomb parts.[97]

The timing of the first mission was dictated by the directive delivered to Spaatz by the War Department on July 24 to undertake a raid after August 3, but it depended on the weather. Not until August 4 did the meteorological outlook improve. A day was needed to prepare the bomb, check the components, and load it into the B-29, christened at the last moment *Enola Gay* after Tibbets's mother. A British representative, Group Captain Leonard Cheshire, was sent to Tinian in the hope of being able to witness the bombing, but LeMay refused to allow him on the main flight or on the photoreconnaissance aircraft that followed. Cheshire thought the American attitude stemmed either from resentment at British participation in an American project or from a more sinister desire to maintain a nuclear monopoly—though he did get to fly on the mission to Nagasaki three days later.[98] At the base the army chaplain blessed the crew and called on God's strength and power so that "armed with Thy might, may they bring this war to a rapid end."[99] At 2:45 a.m. on August 6 (August 5 in Washington), the aircraft took off. The flight was uneventful and the bomb was dropped at 8:15 in the morning over a city waking up for work. The air-raid siren was turned off because only a single aircraft was detected.

The bomb worked just as it was supposed to. It exploded 1,800 feet above ground, destroying all life within a radius of 1.5 kilometers from the hypocenter, burning those within 5 kilometers, followed by a blast wave that tore off the skin and damaged the internal organs of those who survived the initial radiation then briefly by a hurricane-force wind. The thermal radiation up to 500 meters from the hypocenter was 900 times more searing than the sun. The ionizing radiation released left survivors to die a slow death from vomiting and diarrhea and bleeding from the bowels, gums, nose, and genitals.[100] There followed a firestorm generated partly by the primary impact of the bomb but chiefly from secondary fires from stoves, lamps, broken gas mains, and electrical short circuits caused by the blast effects. The fire provoked a wind of 30–40 miles an hour, burning out the whole city center. Only sixteen pieces of firefighting equipment survived the blast; 80 percent of the city's firemen were killed or injured. The fire burnt itself out by early evening as it reached the less built-up outskirts of the city.[101] The firestorm contributed to the destruction of 92 percent of the buildings in the city. The scale of destruction hampered rescue and relief operations, which began on a large scale only by August 9. The injured and dying could not be moved because there were no trains or vehicles; there was a shortage of the necessary medical supplies; and in the first hours there was no water to give to the parched victims.

The impact on the ground dwarfed even the horrors of the Tokyo conflagration. Within 1.5 kilometers of ground zero, some entire bodies were vaporized or their bones turned to charcoal by the intense heat—briefly as hot as the center of the sun—while soft organs boiled away.[102] The blast added a new wave of injuries from flying glass, stones, and wood, even from grass. Tsutomu Yamaguchi was horrified by the sight of five shivering boys: "Blood was pouring in streams from deep cuts all over their bodies, mingling with their perspiration, and their skin was burned deep red, like the colour of cooked lobsters. At first it seemed, strangely, that their burned and lacerated backs and chests were growing green grass! Then I saw that hundreds of blades of sharp grass had been driven deep into their flesh . . . by the force of the blast."[103] The stories of those who survived mirror this horror. Many of those injured in the initial flash and blast were too weak to escape the firestorm and were carbonized by the flames like the crowds in Tokyo. For those further from the hypocenter, there was the dreadful sight of victims staggering away from the fire. Nakamura Setsuko was a thirteen-year-old schoolgirl, rescued from a collapsed building by a soldier while her classmates burned to death. She joined a trail of "ghostly figures" making for the hills: "They did not look like human beings. Their hair stood straight up; their clothes were tattered or they were naked. All were bleeding, burned, blackened, and swollen. Parts of their bodies were missing, flesh and skin hanging from their bones, some with eyeballs hanging in their hands, and some with their stomachs burst open, their intestines hanging out."[104] Setsuko's sister and niece were burnt to a cinder, one aunt and two cousins were found as skeletons, and her uncle and his wife died ten days later, their bodies covered in purple patches, their internal organs dissolving. These are familiar and horrifying descriptions of the raw biological impact of the bomb from those who survived. The number of dead remains disputed, not least because thousands died in the months following the blast from the immediate radiation effects. The Hiroshima City Survey Section calculated by the end of 1946 the death of 118,661 civilians, 112,711 from within two kilometers of the hypocenter. An estimated 20,000 soldiers also died stationed in the nearby castle, giving a total of approximately 140,000, the figure presented by the Hiroshima city authorities to the United Nations in 1976.[105]

News of the successful detonation of the first nuclear bomb reached President Truman on the USS *Augusta* on his way back from the Potsdam Conference. He was lunching with the crew when the message reached him. "This is the greatest thing in history!" he told them. When a telegram followed confirming "results clearcut successful in all respects," he told the assembled officers and crew what had happened. In his memoirs, Truman confessed that he could not keep back his expectations "that the Pacific war might now be brought to a speedy end."[106] Oppenheimer heard the news in a radio broadcast in the evening of August 5, American time, and at Los Alamos there was a renewed round of celebration that the science worked as the scientists hoped it would. The British embassy in Washington reported that the psychological impact on the public "was greater than anything America had experienced in the war, even Pearl Harbor. . . . The lurid fantasies of the comic strips seemed suddenly to have come true."[107] After the detailed news had reached Washington, Groves contacted LeMay on Guam to offer his congratulations and appreciation. Groves prepared the presidential statement with the help of the journalist William Laurence, and it was broadcast by Truman from the *Augusta* at 11:00 a.m. on August 6. The statement threatened yet more destruction if Japan failed to accept the Potsdam ultimatum.

The scientific triumph, pursued by Oppenheimer and his team, was presented as the central feature in Truman's statement: "What has been done is the greatest achievement of organized science in history. It was done under high pressure and without failure."[108] Churchill had prepared a similar broadcast, together with his replacement as prime minister, Clement Attlee, though it was unmistakenly Churchillian: "The whole burden of execution constitutes one of the greatest triumphs of American—or indeed human—genius of which there is a record." Churchill too hoped it would bring the war with Japan to a speedy end.[109] Among the many reasons given for the decision to use the bomb, the scientific and technical achievement in producing and using the first nuclear device deserves a fuller place. The kudos attached to solving the challenge and demonstrating the outcome to the wider world shielded scientists and decision-makers from the harsh reality of what a bomb could do. In August 1945, a report on the Manhattan Project by the Princeton physicist Henry DeWolf Smyth, made public at Groves instigation, focused almost entirely on "the greatest scientific news story of all time."[110] Later both Allied leaders came to view the bomb differently. In 1948, Truman told David Lilienthal, head of the Atomic Energy Commission, "You have got to understand that this isn't a military weapon. It is used to wipe out women and children and unarmed people, and not for military uses."[111] In his final speech to the House of Commons on March 1, 1955, by which time the Soviet Union also possessed the bomb, Churchill memorably described the nuclear age as "the hideous epoch in which we have to dwell. . . . Safety will be the sturdy child of terror, and survival the twin brother of annihilation."[112]

CHAPTER 4

Surrender: The "Sacred Decision"

Our people placed too much confidence in the empire
and held England and America in contempt. Our military
placed too much emphasis on spirit and forgot science.... If
we had continued the war, I would not have been able to
protect the Three Sacred Treasures of the Imperial House,
and [more] people would have been killed. I swallowed my
tears and tried to save the Japanese race from extinction.

—EMPEROR HIROHITO TO PRINCE
AKIHITO, SEPTEMBER 6, 1945[1]

EMPEROR HIROHITO'S EXPLANATION TO HIS YOUNG SON
about why Japan had to give up the war reads oddly for a Western
audience. Protection of the imperial treasures, passed from emperor
to emperor for 2,600 years, was nonetheless a priority but not an

excuse to cover the failure of Japan's hubristic war effort. One of the problems for historians who are keen to demonstrate the direct cause and effect of the bombing of Japan in securing surrender is to grasp the nature of the culture, social values, and political behavior of the Japanese Empire and its leaders. For all Japanese efforts to imitate and learn from the West in the seventy-five years since the founding of the Meiji era in 1868, Japan remained a fundamentally different society and polity from the enemies it faced in the Second World War.

There is no clearer evidence of that difference than the willingness of Japanese servicemen to fight to the death rather than surrender and to attempt suicide if capture was unavoidable. American troops found this behavior bizarre, but it stemmed from a system rooted in worship of the emperor as the father of his people and a living god. Japanese soldiers, sailors, and airmen had an obligation to the emperor to die defending him. Death was not final in this culture. The dead became "warrior-gods" [*gunshin*] enshrined in the Yasukuni Shrine in Tokyo alongside the imperial ancestors, existing as spirits to protect ancient Japan and the Yamato race that inhabited it.[2] This imperial polity was defined as the *kokutai*, a word with no easy translation, invoking both the imperial system and the national body; "sacred homeland" conveys the sense intended and was used in a translation of a volume describing the last day of the war that was prepared by the Japanese Pacific War Research Society in 1968.[3] The imperial house [*kōtō*] was the central institution, responsible for safeguarding the Three Sacred Treasures (mirror, sword, and jewel) handed down over the centuries as a symbol of imperial Japan and its unique civilization. Under the constitution established in 1868, the emperor was the supreme sovereign and military commander in chief, but he was above daily politics and military affairs, which were left to the cabinet and the military high command. For the emperor to intervene rather than approve a course of policy, it was necessary for him to announce a "sacred decision" [*seidan*], but this was a rare occurrence. The very term conveys the cultural gap that existed between the two sides. It was the arcane nature of imperial protocol that made such a decision difficult to make, a fact little understood by American leaders who sought a quick end to the war.

Surrender was in this culture a foreign concept, and Japan had never had to do it. For thousands of years Japan had not been invaded; in the wars against China in the 1890s, with tsarist Russia in 1904–1905, and against Germany in the First World War, Japan had emerged victorious. Japan's expectation in the long war with China that began in 1937, then the war against the British Empire, the United States, and the Netherlands from 1941, was that of "certain victory" [*hisshō*]. Even by 1945 the official media talked only of a final or decisive victory [*kessen*] in defense of the home islands. Talk of surrender was forbidden. The term "end the war" [*shūsen*] could not be used in front of the emperor or in public discourse but instead the euphemism "change of direction." Japanese Navy and Army communiqués turned every defeat in the Pacific into a victory. The Battle of Leyte Gulf in the Philippines in October 1944 saw the final eclipse of the Japanese Navy, but news media in Japan hailed the battle as a triumph: "In hot pursuit of the beaten enemy: Greater war results expected."⁴ The emperor was seldom presented with the truth, although a glance at a map would have told him all he needed to know. It was nevertheless the case that even by summer 1945, most of Japan's colonial territory and the new conquests in China and Southeast Asia were still in Japanese hands, and there were millions of men under arms and undefeated. Nor had any enemy soldier set foot on Japan's homeland.

In these circumstances, the call for unconditional surrender, defined in the Potsdam Declaration, seemed unrelated to the situation facing Japan. Capitulation had no precedent, and to achieve it required a political process centered on the emperor and his willingness or not to give his "sacred decision" with all its constitutional complexities. Some American diplomats who had served in Japan, including the last ambassador, Joseph Grew, understood that Japan was in many ways a parallel universe in which a clear demand for surrender could not easily be accepted even in the face of a terminal military crisis. The Joint Intelligence Committee warned the chiefs of staff in April that the problem "is one of Japanese psychology, which is not readily appreciated by the Western world. . . . Japanese behavior cannot in the circumstances, therefore, be predicted with assurance."[5] The failure of Japan to give up was assumed by many American leaders to indicate a fanatically united people who would rather commit national suicide than surrender, but the Japanese propaganda slogans of "100 million slashing into the heart of the enemy" or "100 million as a suicide squad" was a front only.[6] The Japanese war effort was shot through with divisions, between navy and army over issues of strategy, between different army factions over the nature of the state and economy, and between those of the elite who wanted peace and those who would fight on. The difficulty was not to break down the mythical suicidal union of leaders and led, but to create conditions that would allow a consensus for capitulation to emerge from an otherwise disunited and uncertain leadership.

THE PRINCIPAL DIVISION THAT emerged in the last year of the war lay between those, chiefly in the Japanese Army, who wanted to fight to the very end even if that meant national suicide, and those who searched for some way of terminating the war. For much of the period the emperor evidently favored termination, but for both sides the priority was to preserve the *kokutai* at all costs. The arguments among Japan's leaders revolved around how that might be achieved—by violence, negotiation, or submission. The army began preparations to resist invasion in the autumn of 1944. By spring 1945, the shape of operation "*ketsu-gō*" ("Decisive Operation") had been laid down with two major army commands, one for north and central Honshū, one for western Honshū and the southern islands of Shikoku and Kyūshū. Aircraft, a total of more than 5,000, whatever their condition, were stored away for suicide attacks when the invasion began. The population was expected to participate in repelling the enemy by using whatever weapons they could, from bamboo spears to garden tools. Each soldier and civilian was expected to kill at least one American before they, too, were killed. There would be honor in death and defeat, a "spiritual victory" as the whole population became imbued with the *kamikaze* outlook. The Japanese media were dismissive of German surrender in May 1945. "They gave up like cowards," ran an editorial in the illustrated paper *Asahi Gurafu*, "because they were spiritually flawed."[7] The Japanese Foreign Ministry declared that Germany had violated the agreement in the treaty of December 11, 1941, not to negotiate a separate peace and broke off diplomatic relations. On May 25, 1945, the German embassy burned down in a major incendiary raid on Tokyo.[8]

Those elements in the military leadership who wanted to fight the final battle were supported by a section of the political elite who saw mass mobilization and defiance as the means to create in Japan and its empire a new social and economic order—a renovation, as they called it. They believed that radical change was the key to a decisive victory, which would in turn create conditions for a negotiated peace. Their chief representative was Kishi Nobusuke, a former minister who had helped to transform Japan's war economy. He was supported by a coterie of reform bureaucrats and soldiers who wanted firmer state control of the economy, the mobilization of the entire population, and a "renovationist" nationalism based on the New Order ideology of the conquered wartime area, which saw Japan as the dominant core of an anti-Western pan-Asian territorial bloc. Admiral Kobayashi Seizō, the president of the Imperial Rule

Assistance Association, established in October 1940 to merge the political parties into a common wartime front, wanted to establish a mobilization structure for the entire population under the title "Decisive battle system" that mirrored the ideas of Kishi and his supporters. On March 11, 1945, the day after the bombing of Tokyo, Kishi founded the National Defense Brotherhood to unite the "renovationist" movement. Among his ideas was to use the bombing as the opportunity to encourage a collectivist mentality among the workforce, who would form production armies to move industry and food supplies to mountainous redoubts "where the enemy does not usually bomb." Kishi and his allies among the radical young officers of the Bureau of Military Affairs, who wanted to declare martial law, contemplated overthrowing the government if the call for the final apocalyptic battle was challenged.[9]

What was known of these preparations and propaganda contributed to the view of the Western Allies that the Japanese population and forces would fight to the end with suicidal determination. Henry Stimson warned President Truman in a letter on July 2, 1945, that invasion would prompt "a much more bitter finish fight than in Germany."[10] Little was known of the alternative view among an important element of Japan's political and military leadership that the war should be terminated, an outlook expressed with growing urgency as the external and internal circumstances facing the nation deteriorated in the final year of war. Where this alternative is acknowledged by historians, it has often been regarded as insubstantial or ambiguous, confirming the argument that Japan was never prepared to surrender prior to the atomic bombs. Although there is evidently a difference between accepting unconditional surrender and a desire to terminate the war with at least some conditions, dismissing these efforts ignores a long period before the atomic bombs, even before the major raid on Tokyo in March 1945, in which finding a way to circumvent military intransigence and end the war one way or another was a serious ambition for the peace faction among Japan's political and military leadership. The project for terminating the war was complex and politically delicate, but it paved the way for the eventual "sacred decision" taken in the second week of August not to surrender—a term that remained anathema to Japan's leaders—but to terminate the war on Allied terms.

The evolution of a desire for peace among an important element of the elite can be traced back to at least autumn 1944 or even earlier. Their views were neither uniform nor necessarily coherent, as might be expected in the face of rapidly changing circumstances and fear for the future. During the summer of 1943—the date is uncertain— Emperor Hirohito had hoped for an early end to the war, if it could follow at least one victory to secure a better negotiating position and salvage some degree of national honor, a view he continued to hold up to the summer of 1945 and the battle for Okinawa. At the Imperial General Headquarters, the authors of the daily war journal judged as early as July 1944 that "we can no longer direct the war with any hope of success . . . henceforth we will slowly fall into a state of ruin," followed by a final desperate defense of the homeland."[11] A key figure in the emerging "peace faction" was the navy minister, Adm. Yonai Mitsumasa, who in late August 1944 gave instructions to Rear Adm. Takagi Sokichi to sound out the military and political leadership on "what needs to be done to end the war." Takagi filed regular reports and shared them with two prominent peace advocates, the lord privy seal, Kido Kōichi, and the foreign minister, Shigemitsu Mamoru, both of whom would later play a central part in securing the "sacred decision."[12] In February 1945, Hirohito conducted a series of interviews with the seven *jūshin*, senior advisers to the throne, to seek their counsel on ways to end the war. He found their advice unhelpful—"nobody was able to offer convincing opinions"—but the former prime minister, Prince Konoe Fumimaro, provided a memorial for the throne that highlighted the fears of the conservative elite in Japan that if the war continued there might develop, as in tsarist Russia in 1917, a potentially revolutionary situation, fueled by a conspiracy of communists allegedly concealed in many areas of Japanese society and state. It was this menace, Konoe argued, that made an end to the war more urgent: "both conditions external and internal to Japan are rapidly progressing towards a communist revolution."[13] In such circumstances, the preservation of the *kokutai* for Konoe and for other conservatives was an immovable imperative.

Fear of an internal crisis had a long pedigree among Japan's political and security elite, matched by fear that at some point the communist Soviet Union might use the war to introduce communism into Japan.[14] The civil police and the Special Higher Police Thought Section (established in 1927 to root out any sign of dissent or treason against the empire) devoted much effort both before and during the war to uncovering communist activity where none in reality existed. When the intellectual magazine *Chāō Kōron* failed to honor Army Day in 1943, the Special Police suspected that the editors were Marxists and arrested them and another sixty writers, beating three of the staff to death and putting the rest on trial. Confessions were regularly extorted by torture and used to confirm the need for vigilance against a hidden enemy.[15] Konoe was warned in 1944 by the head of the Tokyo Special Police that communist infiltration represented a "pile of dry hay that would flare up as soon as anyone set a match to it." In August 1944, the Special Police monthly report highlighted four ways in which communists now operated: in contact with communists abroad, in attempts to refound the Japanese communist party (broken up in the 1930s), in work for organizations such as publishing houses, and concealed in war industry.[16] Special attention was given to young workers, whose behavior worried the authorities enough to encourage programs of "daily life guidance" and military-style discipline.[17] Manifestations of popular dissent from the war effort were not widespread, but they prompted anxiety among an elite that was profoundly anticommunist and worried that the demands of total war might provoke social breakdown. This view took on an increased urgency once the urban bombing campaign began and millions of city evacuees undermined social stability in the small towns and villages in which they arrived. The authorities banned the distribution of city newspapers to rural areas, but refugees brought the news with them, spreading fear and criticism of the military.[18] The anxiety over an internal crisis ran as a thread through the discussions around ending the war down to the eventual "sacred decision" in August 1945.

The search for an end to the war gathered pace in early March 1945 at the same time as Curtis LeMay began the indiscriminate incendiary raids that prompted the mass urban exodus. Shigemitsu noted in a memorandum written to himself that Hirohito understood Japan must take measures to conclude the war even at the expense of territorial concessions in the overseas empire. The priority was "how to preserve the imperial reign [*kōtō*] and cultivate future of the Yamato race." On March 8, Shigemitsu met with Kido to discuss termination of the war on the basis of capitulation rather than a negotiated peace. The following day, Kido talked over the situation with the emperor, who, according to Shigemitsu's diary, expressed his desire for the foreign minister to "contemplate ways to end the war," although he was unhappy with the idea of punishing Japan's military leaders as war criminals and the disarmament of Japan, which were known to be Allied conditions. A week later, he visited the ruins of Tokyo and early the following month approved the aging Adm. Suzuki Kantarō as prime minister and Tōgō Shigenori as foreign minister, both expected to play a part in securing peace. In early May, after defeat on Okinawa seemed certain, Kido confided in Konoe that the emperor was more determined than ever on ending the war, and although he worried that disarmament would allow a Soviet invasion, he was now willing to accept both that and the punishment of war criminals. According to Takagi's record of the talk, Kido confirmed that Hirohito was now thinking "the sooner we act, the better." The peace faction understood that the only thing that would terminate the war, given the intransigence of the army leadership, was an imperial *seidan*, and discussion of how to bring this about dated from the spring of 1945 rather than the first weeks of August.[19] The only major condition insisted on by all conservative opinion was survival of the throne and protection of the *kokutai*. Whether this was compatible with Allied intentions was unclear.

This uncertainty was shared in the United States. It was not clear what President Roosevelt had intended when he announced unconditional surrender at the Casablanca Conference in January 1943, but Truman promised on taking office to maintain the commitment absolutely.[20] The State Department had been divided since 1942 between those who favored a "soft peace," which would allow the retention of the imperial system, and those who argued in favor of an uncompromising defeat, even the abolition of the monarchy. There was the question whether surrender meant just the armed forces or the nation as represented by the emperor. The territorial conditions were also ambiguous. At the Cairo Conference in December 1943, the Allies had decided that Japan should relinquish all territory taken by "violence and greed," but whether this included Korea and Taiwan, both acquired before the First World War, was open to question.[21] Those who favored retaining the emperor saw him as a potential source of stability amidst the postwar chaos of a defeated country, even the threat of a communist uprising.

These ambiguities remained unresolved by the summer of 1945 and were reflected in a critical response from the United States' media over the whole issue. Because the priority for the American public was to end the war quickly, the surrender policy was closely scrutinized to see whether there was room for maneuver in concluding the war. "What we are suggesting, to be sure," ran an editorial in the *Washington Post* in May, "is conditional surrender. What of it? Unconditional surrender was never an ideal formula." Another newspaper argued for terms that were "stern, definite, but acceptable" to the Japanese to speed up the war's end. The Japanese Foreign Ministry monitored the American press debate to try to understand whether unconditional surrender really would be unconditional. On July 21, a spokesman for the Office of War Information, Capt. Ellis Zacharias, gave a broadcast on unconditional surrender in which he suggested that afterward, Japan would enjoy "all the benefits laid down by the Atlantic Charter," which included self-determination and equal access to the world market. The suggestion provoked the Japanese news agency, Dōmei, to respond that if the United States was sincere about the offer, "the Japanese military would automatically, if not willingly follow in the stopping of the conflict."[22] Press criticism and the unauthorized broadcast by Zacharias (who had his status as an official spokesman rescinded four days later) almost certainly strengthened James Byrnes's hand in persuading Truman to publish the Potsdam Declaration on July 26, but even that document was less than clear about what the future of the imperial institution would be or whether the surrender was for the military to submit to or the civilian government or both. Kido and the emperor assumed that the wording of the ultimatum allowed the survival of the *kokutai*, which might make acceptance easier to bear.[23]

BY JUNE 1945, the Japanese Empire had reached a terminal crisis. The relentless bombing, which reached a fresh crescendo that month, intensified conservative fears of social crisis. The defeat on Iwo Jima, the loss of Okinawa, and the strong possibility of an invasion of Kyūshū in the near future could not be masked by the military, although the official media hailed Okinawa as a victory because of the heavy cost inflicted on the invaders. It is an irony, therefore, that the brief conference called with the emperor on June 8 by the Supreme War Leadership Council laid down a "Fundamental Policy for the Conduct of the War," which insisted on the army minister's maximum demand for a fight to the end. The council had met on June 6 to draw up the policy at the army's insistence, and the meeting with Hirohito lasted only fifteen minutes, in which the emperor said little. In his postwar "Monologue," recorded in 1946 but made public only in 1990, Hirohito recalled that he found the conference "really strange" because the decision to fight on was evidently "on the surface," while "in their heart of hearts the central [military] authorities were for peace."[24] It seems likely that the peace-faction members of the council—Yonai, Tōgō, and a hesitant Suzuki—were wary of confronting the military leadership in case it prompted a military coup, even their assassination, as Kishi and his supporters wanted. A group of Konoe's advisers had already been arrested in April on suspicion of defeatist activities. Suzuki himself had narrowly survived an assassination attempt in 1936, which may well explain his caution in challenging the army leadership. The need to handle the army with care was a constant brake on the efforts of the peace party.[25]

The reality of Japan's fragile position was brought home by a cabinet annual report on the "State of the Nation's Strength" presented at the same conference with the emperor on June 8. The report in August 1944 had already indicated in stark terms that national strength "was in a downward trend." The report in 1945 highlighted the dangers now faced on the Japanese home front and the hopelessness of continued resistance: in typically euphemistic language, the report concluded that "continuing a modern total war effort was extremely difficult."[26] The value of munitions production between January and August was a fraction of the quantity produced in 1944,

3,226 million yen against 13,170 million yen the year before. The report claimed that by the end of the year, the shipment of goods into Japan would in all likelihood reach zero, while steel production would be cut by three-quarters, and rail transport would be half the level it was in 1944. The "systematic administration of the war economy" would be paralyzed by the naval blockade and the bombing.[27] These problems were exacerbated by the "Empire" bombing program that targeted the smaller towns where industry had been dispersed and made it difficult to hold together the workforce needed to maintain output. The report also highlighted the problem of feeding the population adequately in the context of deteriorating transport, falling imports, and the decline of domestic production. Famine conditions were viewed as a strong possibility.

Food supply deteriorated rapidly in 1945. The overall index of agricultural production (farming, fishing, and forestry) fell from an average of 100 in 1934–36 to 65.4 in 1945, a year of poor rice harvests. The farms lacked labor, fertilizer, and machinery.[28] Production of the major staples—rice, sweet potato, wheat, barley—was 9.9 million metric tons in 1945 but had been 14.6 million metric tons in 1939. The rice ration was maintained until 1945, but the rice was heavily adulterated with potato and other cereals, while the supply of livestock products and vegetables was reduced to a trickle for those who remained in the cities. The black market flourished, despite the efforts of the Economy Police to suppress it, but access to the market was unequal, available only for those who could afford it. By 1945, black market prices were 100 times higher than prices in 1938. Popular resentment was widespread by the summer, evident in the wartime slogan "empty bellies cannot fight a war."[29] Peasants and merchants found ways of hoarding supplies in anticipation of further price rises, aggravating already severe shortages. For the population forced to work long hours, the average supply of 1,600 calories of basic foodstuffs per day was insufficient to maintain health. The demands on labor were strenuous; there were no rest days but a week, so a current complaint claimed, that was "M M, T, W, T, F F."[30] In the bombed cities and for the evacuees who fled them, the food situation was worse. The young Takamizawa Sachiko, mobilized to produce military balloons, worked twelve-hour shifts standing in cold halls with too little to eat; almost one-tenth of the school graduates mobilized with her for the work died of cold, malnutrition, and exhaustion.[31]

Kido took the opportunity of the cabinet reports in June to warn Hirohito that the food crisis might mean that "the [domestic] situation will be beyond salvation." The memorandum on national power presented at the June 8 meeting with the emperor observed that "criticism of the military and government has increased. This trend is apt to shake faith in the leadership class. This is also a sign of the deterioration of public morale."[32] Antiwar graffiti, even slogans hostile to the emperor, multiplied in the course of 1945: "rumors, scribblings, and manifestations are numerically increasing," ran a report from the Special Higher Police. A memorandum for the government from the police in July on "The Shake-Up of Morale as Air Raids Worsen" showed that the regular bombing of small towns, initiated from June onward, had provoked "feelings of terror" that were spreading nationwide.[33] "Everything considered," wrote one young girl, Ezaki Tsuneko, in her diary in July, "I wish I had ended up dying during the bombings. If only there weren't a war."[34] Hirohito, according to Kido in a postwar affidavit, "grieved that many medium and small towns were reduced to ashes by bombing attacks one after another in quick succession." Immediately following the June 8 imperial conference that endorsed the final battle for the homeland, Kido produced a memorial for the throne designed to exploit his knowledge of the emperor's concern for what was happening on Japan's home front. Titled "A Working Plan to Terminate the War," Kido hoped to get the government to seek the emperor's decision to terminate the war while at the same time to agree to send a formal invitation to another power—the Soviet Union was the most probable, because it was not at war with Japan—to mediate for peace in the Pacific war on terms the Allies might well accept. Kido met Hirohito for thirty minutes on June 9 to recommend his plan and was instructed to act as soon as possible.

The idea of using the Soviet Union as the path to the Western Allies for ending the war solidified over the next two weeks, and on June 18 the Supreme War Council convened again at Hirohito's request to overturn the declaration of a war to the end made on June 8 in favor of an approach to Moscow. By then Hirohito had received detailed reports on the crisis in the war economy and the poor state of defenses against an invasion. "Shovels," he later recalled, "are apparently being made of steel used in bombs dropped by the enemy, a fact that shows it is impossible to continue the war."[35] On June 22, the day the battle for Okinawa ended in defeat, an imperial conference was called to endorse the search for a diplomatic exit from the war, but Hirohito took the opportunity to press on the civilian and military leadership the urgency of the moment: "Conditions internal and external in Japan grow tense and the war situation is very difficult, and will likely become more difficult as air raids intensify in future.... I expect that all efforts be made promptly to terminate the war."[36] Kido may well have been reminded of the Japanese approach to the United States in 1905 to help end the Russo-Japanese War, which had resulted in diplomatic agreement. It was decided that the use of Sweden or the Vatican or Switzerland as an intermediary would not work, although informal efforts to find ways to end the war had been floated in all three during the previous year. The Apostolic Delegate in Tokyo was approached in December 1944 by industrialists anxious for a compromise peace; the military attaché in Stockholm, Maj. Gen. Makato Ono, tried to elicit the support of the Swedish king, Gustav V, to make a royal appeal ("a wish of the king") to his fellow monarch, Hirohito. Cdr. Fujimura Yoshirō in Berlin contacted the United States OSS representative in Switzerland, Allen Dulles, to see what chance there was of a negotiated settlement; the Japanese ambassador in Bern in July 1945, Shun'ichi Kase, suggested a peace that kept the emperor on the throne as "a safeguard against Japan's conversion to communism." None of these had official sanction and as a result they petered out.[37] By a process of elimination, the choice fell on the Soviet Union, and a week after the imperial conference on June 22, the first formal efforts were begun.

The choice of the Soviet Union as a possible intermediary is not easy to explain, nor did the peace party make clear how it expected the Soviet Union to act with its major allies to achieve a peace settlement. The Soviet Union was an ally of Japan's three principal enemies and was known to be negotiating agreement with China's nationalist leader, Chiang Kai-shek, on the territorial settlement in northern China when the war was over. Soviet territorial and security interests in East Asia were evident if unpredictable and would come at Japan's expense. In April 1945, the Moscow government had abrogated the Neutrality Pact with Japan signed in 1941, with effect from the following April, a clear sign that relations were likely to change for the worse. One reason why the peace party sought Soviet intercession lay in the willingness of the Japanese Army leadership to consider such an approach. Army leaders had discussed the possibility secretly in May under the code name Item X, even though the army in Manchuria, directly facing any potential Soviet threat, had planned all year for ways to defend the empire if or when the Red Army attacked.[38] Japanese leaders could not know it, but on June 27 the Soviet Politburo, the communist party cabinet, approved war with Japan to begin in August 1945. Two days later, the former foreign minister Hirota Kōki met with the Soviet ambassador, Iakov Malik, to discuss a possible nonaggression pact and agreement on the future status of Manchuria as a prelude to seeking Soviet intercession. In this situation, as the Foreign Ministry official Kase Toshikazu put it in a memorandum, seeking assistance from Moscow was "like crossing a dangerous bridge."[39]

The negotiations proved as fruitless as the informal feelers earlier in the year. The government chose a particularly convoluted approach. Stalin was interested in spinning out negotiations so that the Soviet invasion of Manchuria and Korea could take place before any surrender was submitted to the United States and Britain. When Hirota tried to contact Malik after their meeting, the ambassador feigned illness. The Soviet ambassador remained noncommittal as he was instructed to be. On July 7, Hirohito urged Suzuki to adopt a more straightforward approach by sending an emissary with instructions to ask the Soviet government to assist in brokering peace. Three days later, the Supreme War Council agreed to send Prince Konoe, and the Japanese ambassador in Moscow, Satō Naotake, was asked to see whether Stalin would approve an emissary. Tōgō wrote in the same veiled language used in all formal Japanese communication: "The Emperor is greatly concerned over the mounting calamity and sacrifices of the people of the belligerent powers as a result of the recent war. . . . He is extremely reluctant to permit the increased shedding of blood . . . and he desires that peace be restored as soon as possible for the sake of humanity."[40] Satō attempted to get Stalin and the Soviet foreign minister, Vyacheslav Molotov, to agree to meet him, but they refused any initiative, pleading the coming conference in Potsdam. The Soviet gambit foundered, as it was almost certain to do. Stalin showed the correspondence to his Allies, who already had a dossier on possible peace feelers. Japanese efforts were not regarded as serious. There were few concrete proposals and every indication that the Japanese government wanted to negotiate rather than submit. Yet for the peace party, three months of effort to find a formula that would allow "termination of the war" [*shusen*] rather than "capitulation" [*kōfuko*]—a linguistic distinction chosen to avoid the term surrender, unacceptable to the army—was now in the final stage, atomic bomb or not. The Potsdam Declaration had the effect of defining what the "sacred decision" would have to be.

PRIME MINISTER SUZUKI'S ANNOUNCEMENT to the Japanese press on July 27 that the government would adopt the position of *mokusatsu* in response to the Potsdam Declaration has been variously interpreted because the word carries a range of possible meanings. For the United States leadership, it was tantamount to straightforward rejection, but it seems more likely that Suzuki meant "take no notice of" or "pass over in silence" because he understood that the declaration, although fuller in detail, said little different from the Anglo-American Cairo Declaration of December 1943 on the future of Japan. Nor was the declaration formally presented to the Japanese Foreign Ministry, in which case an answer might have been given, but instead was received through an American radio broadcast.[41] The Japanese government was waiting on the possible response from the Soviet Union, which it was told would have to wait until Stalin and the Soviet delegation returned from Potsdam on August 5. Two days later, Satō asked again about the possibility of the Konoe mission coming to Moscow, but again without a result. After Tōgō had explained to Hirohito what the terms of the declaration meant, the emperor told him that he deemed it acceptable in principle.[42] He and Kido thought the terms even generous after the apocalyptic expectations of national extinction that justified the army's determination to fight on; under the terms of the Potsdam ultimatum, it seemed to them that only the armed forces were expected to surrender, but not the emperor as the embodiment of the *kokutai*. Hirohito also believed that the preparations made for defense of the home islands were far from adequate given the strength of the enemy. The public reaction to the declaration, once the details were known, was also positive, for the terms were less harsh than they had anticipated, although some of the text was left out of the published version at the army's insistence, in case it undermined discipline. The peace faction had already realized that major territorial revision, the trial of war criminals, the disarmament of Japan, and occupation in some form, were all unavoidable in any settlement.

In the ten-day interval between the Potsdam Declaration and the first atomic bomb, the American government waited to see whether there would be Japanese acceptance of the ultimatum, though as *Time* magazine observed, the enemy was "not going to answer 'Yes' as soon as they saw the Potsdam terms," nor was Truman going "to win the war in an afternoon."[43] Press views were optimistic that Japan was nearing the point of surrender. When the first atomic bomb was dropped on Hiroshima on August 6, there were popular expectations that surrender must now follow at once. These hopes were disappointed when there was no indication of capitulation. Army intelligence (G-2) in Washington thought the bomb would not be immediately decisive and expected to wait at least another thirty days before Japan reacted. The Army Operations and Plans Division, which had not been informed of the Manhattan Project, drafted a set of six hypotheses on the conditions for the defeat of Japan, chief of which was still the invasion of the Kantō Plain around Tokyo as the most decisive operation possible.[44] To try to force the issue, Japan was subjected to a massive campaign of psychological warfare to warn of future atomic destruction and to urge the population to seek an end to the war. Broadcasts were beamed from Radio Saipan every fifteen minutes throughout the day, a shower of 15 million leaflets was planned to be dropped on a list of forty-seven cities (in the end 6 million were released), together with one-half million Japanese-language papers that illustrated images of the atomic attack.[45] The leaflet "To the Japanese People" warned that the United States now possessed "the most destructive weapon ever devised by man" and asked the Japanese people to "take steps to end military resistance" on the assumption that this was a possibility.[46]

The impact of the bomb on the Japanese leadership was less direct and less significant than Truman (and most later historians) assumed. The two atomic attacks together destroyed only 5 percent of the urban area, conventional bombing the remaining 95 percent. Japanese leaders at first regarded the attack on Hiroshima as an extension of LeMay's campaign, which continued unabated across the period of the two atomic operations with devastating effect. In eight cases out of twenty-five raids, the degree of urban destruction was higher than at Hiroshima. The raid on Toyama on August 1 burned down almost 100 percent of the urban area; on August 5, four more cities were hit and 4.5 square miles destroyed; on August 8, 73.3 percent of the city of Fukuyama and 21 percent of Yawata were destroyed.[47] At first there was uncertain news from Hiroshima over what had caused the damage. On the basis of Japan's very limited program of nuclear bomb research, Japanese scientists had assumed that no country, even the United States, would be capable of producing a bomb within the span of the war. The Japanese Army was skeptical about Truman's claim that the air force had dropped an atomic bomb (a term banned by the Japanese authorities from public use during the war) and informed Tōgō that Hiroshima was destroyed by "a normal bomb of incredible power." The cabinet called for an investigation in case it was possible to lodge a protest about the bombing with the International Red Cross as a violation of the 1925 Geneva Protocol on gas and biological warfare. The protest was duly filed three days later.[48]

The investigation team for the army, led by Gen. Arisue Seizō, included Japan's premier nuclear physicist, Nishina Yoshio, who was invited to confirm whether it was a nuclear explosion or just American propaganda. Other scientists doubted the possibility, but when the team arrived at Hiroshima on the evening of August 7, Arisue told headquarters in Tokyo that a "special-type" bomb had been used, and "special bomb" became the common description. The term "atom bomb" [*genbaku*] remained confined from the public as it had been during the war. Nishina could not arrive until the evening of August 8, and he began his investigation only the following day. The press reported a new type of bomb only on August 9, with details two days later.[49] The theory began to circulate among those involved that the weapon was a "magnesium bomb": aircraft, it was suggested, had spread magnesium in the air during the night and the following day it was ignited, explaining the flash seen over Hiroshima and the widespread fire. Nishina believed it was a nuclear device but told the investigating team it was "either an atomic bomb or some equivalent." Other teams arrived in Hiroshima only later: the Western Japan Army Command unit arrived on August 9, university medical teams on August 10, a War Department survey group only on August 14. Arguments continued while the investigating groups prepared reports for Tokyo. The first one sent late on August 10 came from the Hiroshima Disaster Investigation Group, but it arrived hours after the emperor had made his first "sacred decision." This report from Arisue and Nishina confirmed that an atomic bomb had been used, but a later army report claimed it was either atomic or a weapon of "equivalent destructive power," while a third report still insisted that the United States could never have found enough uranium.[50] The debate continued over the following week. After the second bomb fell on Nagasaki, the army announced that the bomb was "not formidable" and could be coped with like the fire raids.[51] A further report on August 13 detailed the damage from the "special bomb" but suggested such attacks were survivable with better shelter accommodation and protective clothing. On August 15, the Sixth Army Research Division organized a debate over whether the two bombs were indeed nuclear devices. The "Report on the Hiroshima Catastrophe" the same day still raised doubts: "If the claims that the bomb was an atomic bomb are true . . ."[32]

Well before the attack could be confirmed, Tōgō convened a cabinet meeting at which he was told to wait until the formal scientific report was available. Hirohito was informed and used the additional news to repeat the desire he had expressed for weeks that the war had to be terminated, but under the existing constitution he was not supposed to make and enforce the decision himself. While awaiting the report on Hiroshima, a second crisis emerged that made acceptance of the Potsdam ultimatum imperative. On August 8, Satō finally achieved an audience with Molotov, where he hoped to continue the search for mediation. After exchanging pleasantries, Molotov invited Satō to sit while he read out a declaration of war beginning the following morning. The news arrived in Tokyo at 4:00 a.m. on August 9. The peace faction met at Tōgō's house and agreed that the Potsdam ultimatum should be accepted at once; the group then visited Suzuki, who accepted the same argument: "the Soviet entry into the war meant the collapse of peace negotiations through Soviet mediation, the most important policy of the cabinet."[33] The prime minister recalled after the war that for him the bomb was "an additional reason" to accept defeat, but not the only one.[54] The invasion opened the possibility that the Soviet Union might reach and occupy the Japanese homeland before the Americans, bringing communism in its wake and exploiting the domestic crisis in Japan to win support. The northern island of Hokkaido was defended only by two understrength divisions whose preparations for defense were on the east of the island, facing an American threat, not facing the possible trajectory of the Red Army.[55]

The Soviet declaration of war, agreed with the Western Allies

Young Japanese pilots are given a last glass of sakè before departing for a *kamikaze* suicide mission. The Japanese people were told to adopt the "*kamikaze* outlook" in preparation to repel invasion. *(CBW / Alamy Stock Photo)*

A street in the Philippines capital of Manila littered with corpses after Japanese soldiers and sailors went on a rampage of killing in March 1945 as Allied forces closed in. The atrocity contributed to the American view that the Japanese people deserved what they got in 1945. *(CPA Media Pte Ltd / Alamy Stock Photo)*

Women working at the control panels of the huge plant at Oak Ridge, Tennessee, where uranium separation was undertaken for the atomic bomb program. An estimated 200,000 people worked on the many aspects of the Manhattan Project. *(CBW / Alamy Stock Photo)*

A view of the bleak Los Alamos complex in New Mexico where Oppenheimer and his team lived and worked for two years while preparing the two atomic bombs, "Little Boy" and "Fat Man." *(P.D. Enhanced / Alamy Stock Photo)*

Haywood Hansell (left) and Curtis LeMay (right) pose in front of a B-17 bomber of the Eighth Air Force in 1943. Both men would go on to command the Twenty-First Bomber Command based in the Marianas, where LeMay replaced Hansell in January 1945. *(piemags / Alamy Stock Photo)*

J. Robert Oppenheimer (center left) and Gen. Leslie Groves (center) inspect the remains of the metal tower that housed the test bomb at Alamogordo base on July 16, 1945. The tower was vaporized by the bomb. *(RBM Vintage Images / Alamy Stock Photo)*

Emperor Hirohito on March 18, 1945, surveying the ruins of Tokyo after the firebombing eight days before. The city bombing encouraged him to find ways to terminate the war. *(Photo 12 / Alamy Stock Photo)*

A pile of charred corpses in Tokyo after the conflagration that killed more than 80,000 people on the night of March 9–10 in the most congested residential areas of the capital. *(Nida Picture Library / Alamy Stock Photo)*

A rare photograph of the firestorm that followed the explosion of the first atomic bomb over Hiroshima on August 6, 1945. More than 90 percent of the buildings in the city were destroyed or badly damaged. (INTERPHOTO / Alamy Stock Photo)

A picture taken of wounded survivors of the Hiroshima bombing on August 6, 1945. Most were victims of the initial thermal and ionized radiation when the bomb exploded. By the end of 1946, it was estimated that 140,000 had died from the bomb and its aftereffects. (EgoEye / Alamy Stock Photo)

A photograph of the plutonium bomb as it exploded over Nagasaki on August 9, 1945. The image of the mushroom cloud became a symbol of the new atomic age, but here it is seen from ground level. *(World History Archive / Alamy Stock Photo)*

Nagasaki flattened by the strength of the blast from the bomb, which exceeded that at Hiroshima. The ruined Catholic Urakami Cathedral can be seen in the background. The city was home to thousands of Japanese Christians. *(American Photo Archive / Alamy Stock Photo)*

panese officers surrender their swords as a symbol of submission to the victorious Allies. The process of surrender stretched over three weeks from the initial "sacred decision" to terminate the war taken on August 14, 1945. *(Associated Press / Alamy Stock Photo)*

oviet soldiers parade on a tank through the center of the port of Darien (Dalian) on the anchurian coast after rapid victory over Japanese forces in August 1945. The port was on alin's wish list of geopolitical gains from Soviet entry in the war against Japan. *(CPA Media e Ltd / Alamy Stock Photo)*

Technicians work on renovating the B-29 bomber *Enola Gay* for the planned fiftieth anniversary exhibition at the Smithsonian Air and Space Museum in Washington, D.C. The exhibition prompted a major argument over how Americans should remember the Pacific war, and, after protest, the Japanese element was removed. (Dennis Brack / *Alamy Stock Photo*)

Protestors in central Tokyo on January 22, 2021, demanding that the Japanese governme[nt] sign the UN Treaty on the Prohibition of Nuclear Weapons. Antinuclear protest goes ba[ck] to the 1950s when Hiroshima and Nagasaki initiated campaigns for peace and nuclear disa[r]mament. (*Aflo Co. Ltd. / Alamy Stock Photo*)

at Potsdam, was a shock in Tokyo but not unexpected in Manchuria, where the weight of the Soviet offensive was felt. Between May
and August, the Soviet armed forces transferred 403,000 men, 2,119
tanks and self-propelled guns, and 17,374 vehicles to the three Far
Eastern army groups. Much of the transfer was veiled from the Japanese Kwantung Army in Manchuria by deception measures, so that
Japanese military intelligence underestimated Soviet strength by up
to 50 percent. The total Soviet deployment amounted to 1,559,500
troops against a Japanese total of 993,000 in Manchuria and Korea,
but in armor and air power the Soviet side was vastly superior.
Against the 4,600 aircraft of the Red Army, it has been calculated
that the Japanese could employ only 180. Soviet armor comprised
5,556 tanks and self-propelled guns; Japanese tanks numbered 1,155,
but they were small and poorly armed with 37- and 57-mm main
guns almost incapable of knocking out any Soviet armor.[56] Many of
the Japanese troops were drafted in from among men living in Manchuria who had little training or experience of battle. The Japanese
Army units were short of all forms of ammunition, even swords
and bayonets. The invasion when it came exposed the asymmetrical
nature of the conflict. The unexpected mobility and firepower of
the Red Army produced an East Asian version of *Blitzkrieg*. Within
hours the Japanese defensive lines were pierced, bypassed, and overrun. Infantry advanced at an average of thirty to forty kilometers
a day, armored formations at seventy to ninety kilometers.[57] The
Soviet Union was overnight transformed from potential arbiter to a
menacing threat to the future of the empire.

All the factors that had informed the debate on terminating
the war came into play in the day following the onset of the Soviet
invasion—fear of communism, anxiety about domestic stability, the
threat of bombing, conventional as well as atomic, the poor level of
defensive preparations, and the priority to try to preserve the *kokutai* from Allied elimination. There seems no reason to assume that

just one of the ingredients in this cocktail of dangers was regarded as decisive. They all mattered. Hirohito early on the morning of August 9 told Kido to arrange with Suzuki acceptance of the ultimatum. A meeting of the Supreme War Council was called for 10:30 a.m. and the issue opened to debate. No one at the meeting suggested complete rejection of the declaration, but there emerged a clear division over what conditions might be asked for. The army and navy chiefs of staff and the war minister, Anami Korechika, wanted four conditions: retention of the emperor, no occupation, Japan to organize its own disarmament, and to punish any Japanese war criminals. Yonai, Tōgō, and Suzuki favored just one condition, survival of the imperial institution. The group remained deadlocked. At a cabinet meeting called for 2:30 p.m., the deadlock persisted. Yonai, whose desire for peace to avoid a social crisis went back almost a year, told the meeting that he questioned continuing the war "in light of the domestic situation, rather than the atomic bomb and Soviet entry," but the army representatives still wanted four conditions rather than one. At the end of the meeting there were six in favor of accepting the ultimatum, three firmly against, and five who wanted some solution in between.[58]

After the meeting, Kido and Shigemitsu agreed that the final act must now rest with the emperor, who should make a "sacred decision." This was a complex constitutional issue—the cabinet was supposed to have a unanimous decision before meeting the emperor—but Kido persuaded Hirohito that he must intervene, and Hirohito agreed. The cabinet secretary, Sakomizu Hisatsune, arranged for an imperial conference with the Supreme War Council without informing the army and navy leaders in advance, which was against constitutional practice. The conference was called at 11:30 in the evening of August 9, and the deadlock was rehearsed in the presence of the emperor. The meeting was also attended, against precedent but at the emperor's invitation, by the chair of the Privy

Council, Hiranuma Kiichirō, who like Yonai emphasized that the food crisis and domestic unrest were urgent factors in seeking an end to the war on one rather than four conditions. At the critical moment, Suzuki rose and against custom asked Hirohito for his view. The emperor first criticized the military preparations for the final battle, which he defined as inadequate: "there has always been a discrepancy between plans and performance." In his postwar "Monologue," dictated in 1946, he recalled that at this point "I could not comprehend how the imperial capital could be defended or how we could make war."[59] He went on to explain to the assembled council that the number of "air raids is escalating every day," and he did not wish for his people "to fall into deeper distress or destroy our culture." It was, he concluded, time to "bear the unbearable . . . for the sake of the nation" and to accept the Allied ultimatum on the one condition. This opinion, which included nothing on the atomic bomb or on the Soviet declaration of war, was not a formal decision, though it was treated as a *seidan* by the leadership.[60] To be binding it required a separate cabinet decision, and in the early-morning hours of August 10 the cabinet met and quickly endorsed the emperor's view. At dawn, the Foreign Ministry, through Swiss mediation, informed Byrnes that the Potsdam Declaration was accepted so long as it was possible to maintain the "prerogatives of His Majesty as a Sovereign Ruler," an alteration recommended by Hiranuma at the imperial conference.[61]

In the midst of the final crisis, a second atomic bomb was dropped on Nagasaki at just after 11:00 a.m. on August 9, while the Supreme War Council was in session to discuss the terms for acceptance of the ultimatum. The second atomic bomb has generally attracted less scholarly attention, but it also played a minor part in the deliberations of the Japanese leadership, "an appendix" according to Adm. Hoshina Zenshirō, who witnessed the discussions.[62] The use of the plutonium bomb, first tested at Alamogordo, was included in the directive to Carl Spaatz from the War Department on July 24: "Additional bombs will be delivered on the above targets [Kokura, Niigata, Nagasaki] as soon as made ready by the project staff."[63] Truman was not informed, because the military decision to use additional bombs had already been taken. The date was fixed for August 11, but poor weather prospects meant moving the date to the morning of August 9. The target was Kokura with its large arsenal, but the impact on the whole city was expected to be the same as at Hiroshima or even greater given that the blast effects from the plutonium core were expected to be higher than from the uranium bomb.

The B-29 *Bockscar*, piloted by Charles Sweeney, left Tinian early in the morning and arrived over Kokura to find it covered in cloud and smoke from the earlier bombing of Yawata. Sweeney chose the secondary target, Nagasaki, and arrived over the city before 11:00 a.m. to find again a bank of cloud. The cloud parted briefly to allow the bomb to be dropped some way from the aiming point, close to the Catholic Urakami Cathedral. The bomb detonated at an elevation of about 1,500 feet, achieving a massive blast effect and releasing the mushroom cloud whose iconic image has come to define the nuclear age. The journalist William Laurence, who was in the photoreconnaissance aircraft that arrived over Nagasaki, together with Leonard Cheshire and the British scientist William Penney, later described his feelings on watching the mushroom bloom. "The mushroom cloud," he wrote, "was even more alive than the pillar, seething and boiling in a white fury of creamy foam, sizzling upwards and then descending earthward, a thousand 'Old Faithful' geysers rolled into one."[64] The effect on the city was recalled by another journalist invited to fly over Nagasaki when the war was over: "We saw half a city laid waste, not in ruins as after an ordinary bombing or shelling, but smashed flat . . . still stinking of death."[65]

The bomb was less destructive than the bomb on Hiroshima

because of the topography. Nagasaki lay across a system of river valleys with mountains to the east and west, while Hiroshima lay on a flat plain. The blast effects were nevertheless extensive, followed by a firestorm that destroyed everything within two kilometers of the hypocenter. Some 36 percent of the buildings in the city were destroyed, most of them in the Urakami valley district, where blast destruction extended 2.5 kilometers from ground zero. The death toll was lower than in Hiroshima, but by the end of 1945, according to the Nagasaki City Commission, there were 73,884 deaths and injury to a further 74,909.[66] There was less damage to the fire stations in Nagasaki, where only six were destroyed and five pieces of equipment lost, but the destruction to water mains and pipes meant that the fire service could do little to stem the firestorm. On August 8, the rescue and relief system in Nagasaki had discussed how to cope with an atomic attack after receiving news from Hiroshima, but the decision to evacuate schoolchildren the following day came too late. Rescue and medical personnel arrived at the center of the city more rapidly and in larger numbers than in Hiroshima, and the survival of the railway station meant that the injured could be moved to neighboring hospitals, which had not been possible in the first attack.[67] The eyewitness accounts of survivors tell the same story as Hiroshima—piles of burnt corpses, bodies reduced to a residue of charcoal bones, the lines of ghost-like figures escaping the city with sloughed skin, blackened and bloodstained. Matsumoto Fujie searched for her mother, found her bones and ashes, and saw that the pumpkin field in front of her house had been blown clean. Instead of a pumpkin on the field she found a woman's head: "a gold tooth gleamed in the wide-open mouth. A handful of singed hair hung down from the left temple over her cheek, dangling in her mouth. Her eyelids were drawn up, showing black holes where her eyes had been burned out. The head had come right off at the neck."[68]

The bombing of Nagasaki and its aftermath coincided with the final efforts to achieve an imperial decision, but it played no apparent part in reaching it. The site was visited by a team from the military police on August 10 and by a naval team four days later. Nishina Yoshio arrived to survey the bomb damage only on August 14, the same day as the second imperial *seidan*.[69] The bombing did affect Truman and provoked a more ambivalent response from the president and the American public than the bomb on Hiroshima. The secretary of commerce, Henry Wallace, recorded in his diary that at a cabinet meeting on August 10, Truman "said the thought of wiping out another 100,000 people was too horrible. He didn't like the idea of killing, as he said, 'all those kids.'"[70] At the same time, he responded defensively against any criticism. In a letter on August 11 to the clergyman Samuel Cavert, one of the founders of the National Council of Churches, Truman famously responded that in the case of Japan, "When you have to deal with a beast you have to treat him as a beast," although only two days before he had responded to another telegram that even if the Japanese were beasts, he could not believe that "we should ourselves act in the same manner."[71] At the cabinet meeting on August 10, Truman announced that there would be no more atomic bombings, although three days later, still waiting for the Japanese to accept surrender fully, he remarked in a news conference at the White House that "another atomic bomb seemed the only way to hasten the end."[72] Similar ambivalence was reflected in public response to news of the second bomb. The British embassy reported that there was evidence of public anxiety over the human cost: "there is a good deal of heart-searching about the morality of using such a weapon, especially against an enemy already known to be on his last legs."[73] At Los Alamos, the scientists were also disturbed by confronting the reality of what a nuclear bomb had done, although they could have had no doubt about the level of destruction a bomb would produce. The mood of jubilation after Hiroshima evaporated three days later. Oppenheimer was observed in an FBI report to be a "nervous wreck," while another eyewitness recalled a widespread "revulsion" against the costs of bombing Nagasaki, even if it was supposed to end the war sooner.[74]

When on August 13 Truman suggested using a third bomb, this time on Tokyo, there were no bombs yet available, but the threat reflected the frustration felt in Washington at the slow pace of the final negotiations. Marshall had told Groves on August 11 not to ship a third bomb to Tinian, and the decision was confirmed two days later. Groves kept the atomic staff in place on the island in case the surrender turned sour, while the Twentieth Air Force commander drew up a provisional list of seven cities that might be bombed if necessary.[75] The Japanese acceptance of the Potsdam ultimatum on August 10 with a single condition inserted about the prerogatives of the emperor caused a renewal of the argument in Washington over what unconditional surrender ought to mean. State Department views were generally hostile. The director of the Department of Far Eastern Affairs objected that "prerogatives of the emperor includes everything" when the object was to place limits on imperial power. Byrnes, however, wanted a swift agreement. According to one of his assistants, Joseph Ballantine, Byrnes's response to the wording on "prerogatives" was "Oh no, we'll accept that. We've got to accept that just as it stands, because the Army and Navy is [sic] sick of fighting, the President wants to get the surrender over with as fast as possible." He had to be persuaded that the wording should reflect the requirement that the emperor remained subject to the Supreme Commander of the Allied Powers—General MacArthur—while still retaining the throne.[76] When the news of the Japanese provisional acceptance was made public the following day, there was popular belief that the war would now be ended. The *New York Times* headline claimed GIS IN PACIFIC GO WILD WITH JOY: "LET

'EM KEEP EMPEROR" THEY SAY; in Washington the mood was "they can keep their son of heaven" as long as the war ended.[77]

Byrnes's reply to Tōgō was open to interpretation, but Hirohito thought that the wording suggested the survival of the imperial institution and with it the *kokutai*. When it was explained to him on August 12 he was heard to say, "I think the reply is all right. You had better proceed to accept the note as it is." According to the memoirs of Ishiwato Sōtarō, the imperial household minister, Hirohito was willing to broadcast on the radio to his people his imperial rescript on acceptance. Between August 10 and 12, the emperor met with all the *jūshin* and the senior members of the imperial family to explain his decision that followed a string of military defeats and the exhaustion of Japan's resources. The response from Byrnes was nevertheless rejected by the war party, which resented the idea that the emperor would be subject to MacArthur and assumed that this spelled the end of the imperial system. The Foreign Ministry translated "subject" as "placed under the restriction of" to make it less bald, but the army minister, Anami, had it translated as "subordinate to," which was less acceptable. Suzuki had to be persuaded that the American response did not mean the emperor's subjection, but acceptance would make necessary a second *seidan*.[78] The army minister and the two service chiefs of staff preferred to reject the American note and continue the war, though at a meeting with senior army staff on August 10, Anami had made it clear that the emperor's wish to terminate the war was binding, and disobedience would be "over my dead body."[79] In the background, as the peace party feared, radical army officers had been preparing a coup to overturn the decision for peace and rule through martial law. The coup preparations took place from early August. Lt. Col. Takeshita Masahiko drafted a call for martial law, the arrest of government leaders, and seizure of the royal palace. The plotters did not rule out assassination of the main members of the peace party, including Suzuki, Tōgō, Yonai, and Prince Konoe. The chief conspirators from the Bureau of Military Affairs, Lt. Col. Shiizaki Jirō and Maj. Hatanaka Kenji, tried to enlist Anami's support, but despite his hostility to surrender, he remained aloof from the plot.[80]

American frustration at delay stemmed from the failure to appreciate how arcane were Japanese constitutional procedures and how difficult it was to unite a fractured elite. This had little to do with the bombing, conventional or atomic, but was the result of a cultural context in which surrender had no place. Termination of the war or final battle were fundamentally opposed concepts that could not be reconciled, but neither meant surrender. The first "sacred decision" on August 10 had not been enough to end the conflict between the two positions, and on August 13, after Hirohito made clear to Tōgō his willingness to accept the Byrnes note, a cabinet meeting in the afternoon concluded that the following day, Hirohito would be asked to pronounce a second "sacred decision" to accept unconditionally the amended American document. The imperial conference was called on the following morning after Suzuki and Kido asked the emperor to summon it, but once again at short notice to outmaneuver the war faction in the cabinet. At 10:30 on the morning of August 14, the cabinet and the Supreme War Council assembled in the underground shelter of the palace.

The subsequent meeting was, for those attending, a moment of high drama. The underground room was hot and humid. The emperor arrived after twenty-five minutes in a simple military costume and sat in front of the assembly at a small table covered in gold brocade. The cabinet and council sat at long tables at right angles to the emperor, as protocol required. Suzuki first apologized for having to ask for a second *seidan*, then allowed three opponents of acceptance to speak. He then asked for an imperial decision to overcome the cabinet division. There was utter silence in the room. Hirohito then made the historic speech that ended Japan's war. The wording was recorded afterward by the director of information, who cross-checked with others present to produce the best transcript available. The emperor's formulation was archaic but clear enough. He began by claiming that the situation of the world and conditions within Japan made it impossible to continue the war. He believed that the Byrnes reply should be accepted, "And I would like all of you to agree with me." He wanted to avoid a situation in which "the whole country will be reduced to ashes" and to preserve the *kokutai*. Otherwise, he argued, "I will not be able to carry on the wishes of my imperial ancestors." The emperor had tears in his eyes as he spoke; soon the rest of the meeting was, according to testimony, reduced to sobbing aloud. The imperial decision was endorsed by the cabinet later in the afternoon and arrangements made to record the imperial rescript for broadcasting the following day.[81]

The wording made no mention of defeat or surrender. The "sacred decision" was to terminate the war. Nor was there any mention of the suffering inflicted by Japan's violent imperialism on the conquered areas of Asia and the Pacific, only of the emperor's desire to end the suffering of his own people from bombs, hunger, and exhaustion. The reference to imperial ancestors also indicated Hirohito's understanding of his obligation to a Japanese past in which conquest, occupation, and surrender had been avoided and the *kokutai* continuously preserved. A few weeks earlier, Hirohito had told Kido that he worried lest enemy paratroopers should land to seize Imperial Headquarters and the Three Sacred Treasures [*sansha-no-jingi*] held at the Ise and Atsuta Shrines. By the time of the "sacred decision," the prospect of foreign invasion, either Soviet or American, would make it difficult to protect the treasures from sacrilege and the betrayal of his ancestors. In his 1946 "Monologue," he returned to the theme that if the enemy had captured the treasures, there would be "no expectation of preserving them," and as a result it would be difficult to "preserve the *kokutai*." Before that happened, he continued, "I thought we would have to make peace."[82] Exotic as this concern might seem, it should not be disregarded. Hirohito was bound to Japan's mythical imperial culture, which is why accepting an end to the war, which seemed straightforward to the Allied leadership, was not a simple political calculation but one that required a profound psychological engagement with a historic past and an uncertain future. As it was, the second "sacred decision" broke with constitutional tradition. Hirohito later told Grand Chamberlain Fujita Hisanori that "Here for the first time, I was given the opportunity to speak my own opinion freely.... So I expressed my own conviction that I had been holding for some time and ended the war."[83]

A recording of Hirohito's announcement of the imperial rescript was broadcast on the morning of August 15, by which time Washington had been notified of acceptance of the Byrnes note and the Allied ultimatum. In the early hours of the day, the military plotters had stormed the palace and hunted vainly for the recording of Hirohito's announcement. The coup was foiled by the action of forces loyal to the emperor and the palace secured again by 8:00 in the morning. Other soldiers tried, and failed, to storm the broadcasting station. At midday the announcement was made. The broadcast included reference to the "most cruel bomb" now being deployed, perhaps to explain more clearly to his people the inevitability of termination, because it had not featured in his speech the day before. But the message was more generally about avoiding the destruction of Japan because "the general trends of the world have all turned against her interest," an oblique acknowledgement of defeat.[84] The emperor's recording was difficult for many Japanese to understand, partly due to the archaic language he used, partly to poor reception in the ruined cities and distant villages. In Nagasaki, Matsu Moriuchi was cremating the bodies of two relatives and a baby on a small pyre made from fragments of ruined wood when she heard a crowd of people sobbing in the nearby school. A friend went to see what was happening and returned shouting that Japan had surrendered. "The war was over!" Matsu recalled. "I sank down alongside the pyre and sat there, dumb. All I had left was a five-year-old orphan and the bones and ashes of three dead! For these ashes, to have endured the long misery of the war!"[85]

THE "SACRED DECISION" WAS not seen as a surrender in Japan either at the time or since, but the military leadership understood that the imperial proclamation meant the admission of defeat. The day of the imperial broadcast, General Anami cut open his stomach in his office in the tradition of *seppuku*, or ritual suicide. Another eight senior generals and admirals followed suit shortly after the announcement. Suzuki did not commit suicide but resigned the same day to be replaced by Prince Higashikuni, Hirohito's uncle. On August 17, a further effort was made to alter the conditions of the ultimatum by suggesting only certain specified parts of Japan should be occupied, but the American side wanted full occupation, not least to ensure that Stalin did not take advantage of the hiatus to occupy part of the home islands too. The Japanese Empire was geographically dispersed, so that emissaries had to be sent from the emperor to local commanders to assure them that the imperial decision was to give up the war. The terms of occupation and the surrenders across the Japanese Empire were amalgamated in General Order Number One, issued by MacArthur following the surrender ceremony. There were separate surrenders to the British at Singapore, to Chiang Kai-shek's forces at Nanjing on September 9, and the remaining Japanese garrisons in the Pacific surrendered to Admiral Nimitz.

The exception for Japan was the end of the war with the Soviet Union. Fighting continued until September 5 as Stalin's forces sought to seize the territories granted to the Soviet Union at the

Yalta Conference. Moscow did not regard the broadcast on August 15 as a firm capitulation. The Red Army pushed on to capture the main cities of Manchuria and the ports that Stalin hoped to control, while Soviet forces advanced into Korea as far as the 38th Parallel, the demarcation line agreed shortly before with Stalin.[86] Beyond that lay Japan and the northern islands. Japanese leaders had been right to worry about Soviet intentions once invasion began. On August 16, Stalin asked Truman for an occupation zone on northern Hokkaido and a few days later instructed the Soviet representative at MacArthur's headquarters, General Kuz'ma Derevianko, to ask not only for a zone on Hokkaido but also for a zone in Tokyo, like the zones established earlier in the year in occupied Berlin. Stalin had also hoped for a joint supreme command in Japan, even a surrender ceremony with joint American and Soviet signatories. Truman and MacArthur refused all such requests, but the Soviet high command ordered Marshal Aleksandr Vasilevskii to occupy northern Hokkaido and the whole of the Kurile Islands, even though the southern part of the group had been assigned to the United States' zone. One division was detailed for the operation in the Kuriles, two divisions for Hokkaido. Embarkation orders were issued on August 21, but at the last moment Stalin hesitated to defy the United States and canceled the orders.[87] The whole of the Kurile archipelago was nevertheless seized against Japanese resistance, which ended with a final surrender on September 5. The Soviet invasion was in effect a separate war with an ending distinct from the surrender on mainland Japan.

The chief surrender ceremony took place almost three weeks after the imperial rescript, aboard the USS *Missouri* in Tokyo harbor, where the document was signed by Japan's new foreign minister, Shigemitsu Mamoru. After a wave of delighted celebration in the United States at the news in August, there was a growing unease and frustration at what the public saw as deliberate procrastination by the Japanese leadership. A joke circulated in Washington: "Do you think Japan's surrender will shorten the war?"[88] The situation in Japan seemed suspended between the reality of defeat and the onset of postwar normality. In the interval, the Japanese media had already begun to construct the myth of the "sacred decision" as an act of imperial benevolence. The *Nippon Times* on August 15 ran the headline THE RESTORATION OF PEACE above the assertion that "Japan has made this decision which will contribute immeasurably to the future welfare of humanity."[89] The gap between the broadcast and the arrival of the first American soldiers on August 28 allowed protests against the "sacred decision" to continue. Aircraft of the Navy Special Attack Corps (a *kamikaze* unit) dropped leaflets over Tokyo warning "Do not surrender. Do not believe the imperial rescript. It is a false document." Some troops seized hills in the center of Tokyo to challenge the decision, but they dispersed except for one group that committed suicide with hand grenades. Another plot was hatched to seize the imperial palace on August 20, but that too misfired. The Sagamihara Air Corps refused to disarm and threatened to attack American aircraft as they came to land at the Atsugi airfield. Emissaries from the emperor were sent to establish discipline, and the threatened violence was avoided.[90] Nothing indicated more clearly the sacral nature of the emperor's position than the willingness of millions of soldiers to accept his decision rather than fight on.

Two days after the surrender ceremony, Hirohito addressed the reconvened Diet. He described the ending as the "cessation of hostilities" and called upon his people to surmount the hardships of the termination of the war "and make manifest the innate glory of Japan's national polity."[91] The fact that he was still on his throne indicated the extent to which the final surrender was not entirely unconditional, as the peace party had hoped. Despite popular anger in the United States at Hirohito as a war criminal (a Senate Resolution in September 1945 had called unanimously for his arrest), MacArthur saw the emperor as an instrument for stabilizing postwar Japan and succeeded in protecting him from American calls for vengeance. When Hirohito talked of abdication, MacArthur persuaded him against it. In June 1946, the chief prosecutor in the Tokyo International Military Tribunal announced that the emperor would not be subject to arrest.[92]

The long struggle in Japan during 1945 to find a way to terminate the war suggests a different narrative over the impact of the bombing, both conventional and atomic. The Japanese leadership found the idea of unconditional surrender a cultural leap too difficult to make, but there were persistent divisions among the leadership over whether to terminate the war or fight to an annihilating finish that were exceedingly difficult to reconcile even in the face of aerial destruction. The firebombing, which continued remorselessly through to August 14–15, was a central reference point from the early summer onward for those seeking peace, including the emperor, precisely because it intensified the looming social crisis through evacuation, dispersal, and physical destruction and exposed the feebleness of the Japanese armed forces in response. Failure in the ground war also contributed to the final decision, following the loss of Okinawa and the threatened invasion of the southern homeland, though it is often overlooked when explaining the "sacred decision." A Foreign Ministry directive to destroy documents on August 7 was issued because "the Imperial Land will become a war zone."[93] Hirohito on several occasions blamed the armed forces for failing to prepare Japan's defense with any hope of success. The Soviet invasion was a shock because it brought suddenly very near not just the loss of the new empire in Asia to a communist power but also the possibility of Soviet invasion and occupation before the Americans arrived. The atomic bomb on Hiroshima was just one factor in the cocktail of existing pressures on the Japanese leadership, and the detailed report on the raid arrived in Tokyo only after the initial *seidan* had been promulgated. The raid on Nagasaki had less impact, but like the first atomic bomb, it must be factored into a more complex response from the leadership to Japan's situation, not least the fear that the bombing and blockade might prompt revolutionary crisis if Japan's war effort ended like the Russian and German war efforts in 1917–1918. The emperor's postwar reflections both in his "Monologue" and in conversation with Grand Steward Tajima Michiji in the early 1950s returned to the points he made on August 10 and 14—that he wanted to prevent further suffering for his people, for which he felt a strong moral responsibility. But the obverse of that concern was anxiety that the *kokutai* might dissolve through internal crisis rather than external military pressure.[94] The relationship between the surrender of Japan and the impact of the atomic bombs must be set in this broader political and social context; the equation "bombing equals surrender" in the end begs too many questions.

CHAPTER 5

Aftermath

The U. S. Government should admit that its atomic
attacks on Hiroshima and Nagasaki were atrocious
acts violating international law and apologize.

—JAPAN CONFEDERATION OF ATOMIC
BOMB VICTIMS, 1994[1]

The United States owes no apology to Japan for
having dropped the two atomic bombs.

—PRESIDENT BILL CLINTON, APRIL 1995[2]

THE REFUSAL OF PRESIDENT CLINTON TO GIVE AN
apology for the atomic bombing of Hiroshima and Nagasaki was
consistent with the widely held view long after the war that the bombs
were both necessary and legitimate in bringing the war to an end.
President Ronald Reagan approved of an operation in which "more
than one million [American] lives were saved." His successor, George

H. W. Bush, reaffirmed in 1991 that the bombing "spared millions of American lives."[3] The only American president to visit Hiroshima while in Japan was Barack Obama on May 27, 2016, where he spoke at the Peace Park "to mourn the dead, including 100,000 Japanese men, women, and children."[4] His visit proved to be the exception. The tradition was set by President Truman himself. In the draft of an after-dinner speech in December 1945, he claimed that saving a quarter of a million young American lives "was worth a couple of Japanese cities, and I still think that they were and are."[5] In a television interview in 1958, when Truman was asked whether he had any regrets over the bombing, he replied, "not the slightest—not the slightest in the world." In his memoirs he insisted that "he had never had any doubt that it should be used."[6]

The United States authorities in Japan in 1945 were neverthe-less cautious in allowing any dissemination of news or information about the bombings, both conventional and atomic. The priority was to ensure that the raids were not used as the means to accuse the American occupiers of committing atrocities. On August 9, the Office of War Information had already instructed that in any announcement about Hiroshima and Nagasaki, it should be clearly stated that there was "sufficient military character to justify attack under the rules of civilized warfare."[7] Allied press correspondents who tried to publicize what had happened found themselves subject to a rigid censorship. The extent of radiation sickness was a particu-lar issue that the American authorities hoped to conceal. The Asso-ciated Press science correspondent, Howard Blakeslee, publicized the news of Japanese survivors who died days or weeks later from the effects, but Groves and Oppenheimer tried to suppress it. In Sep-tember, Oppenheimer even invited a selection of correspondents to the site of the Trinity test to demonstrate that there was no residual radioactivity, although he and other scientists knew that it was the initial moment of the explosion that created the deadly radiation effects.[8] The Australian journalist William Burchett also tried to highlight the severe aftereffects of the bombs, but his accreditation was withdrawn by the Civil Censorship Detachment and his camera stolen. Reels of film taken of the bomb sites were confiscated by the censors, and every effort was made to eliminate publication in Japan of images and information not only of Hiroshima and Nagasaki but also of the firebombing of Tokyo five months before.[9] Reproduction of photographs of the injured Japanese was prohibited in both Japan and the United States, though one taken for *Life* magazine slipped the net and was published in October 1945. It was approved because the photographer added "that their injuries looked like those he had seen when he photographed men burned at Pearl Harbor," both minimizing the bomb's damage and reminding readers of why the bombing was morally justified.[10]

There was extensive research carried out officially by United States and British teams of scientists, doctors, and economists to judge the effects of both the conventional bombing of Japanese cities and the two atomic bombs. The United States Strategic Bombing Survey produced detailed reports on every aspect of Japanese industry and civil life under the bombs. As in Europe, a British Bombing Survey Unit was created and sent to Japan to carry out a British evaluation, in particular of the effect of the atomic bombing. The American study of the strategic bombing campaign was critical of the target selection and concluded that a systematic attack on inland communications by both the Twenty-First Bomber Command and the U.S. Navy's fleet air arm would "in all probability have led to an earlier surrender." On the urban fire raids, the report concluded that the campaign from June onward against smaller and medium-sized towns had more effect on the Japanese decision to end the war than the major raids earlier in the year.[11] The British Mission report on the bombing also concluded that given the dispersal of Japanese military industry, "even a sketchy but coordinated attack on the railway system" would have brought dispersed production to a standstill—an argument consistent with the effect that the bombing campaign against transportation had had on the German war economy. The British Mission also thought that the urban area attacks had contributed "to the decision of the Japanese not to stay to fight an Okinawa action in the homeland," which the evidence from Japanese records has confirmed.[12]

The two atomic attacks were nevertheless the prime focus of attention. In both the American and the British cases, a central concern was to gauge the effects on British or United States cities if they were subjected to nuclear strikes. The British Bombing Survey team began work before the surrender on September 2 following instructions from the Air Ministry and the Home Office to get data on the effect on air-raid shelters and civil defense that were useful for British postwar planning. The head of the British Research and Experiments Department, Reginald Stradling, who had advised on bombing Germany, produced a plan to survey atomic bomb damage. "The fundamental aim," ran his report, "is to estimate the resistance to this [the atomic bomb] and similar bombs of the various kinds of building which might house people in Great Britain, now and in the future."[13] A survey of Nagasaki sent to Groves and James Chadwick in September emphasized the staggering blast effects on houses so flimsy compared with the model village at the Dugway Proving Ground that the contrast was "ludicrous." A report produced by the British Mission in December 1945 suggested that if a similar atomic bomb were dropped on a British urban area of average building density, up to 115,000 houses would be damaged and 50,000 killed. The overall picture, the report concluded, is "sombre." Means of protection against a nuclear attack "present a formidable problem."[14]

The Manhattan Engineer District produced its own lengthy report on the effect of the two bombs, finally distributed in June

1946, which again focused on the blast effects and damage to various forms of construction. By this time, the discussion of the effects on the population included acknowledgment that the first minute of the explosion was responsible for the death and injuries caused by radiation at the time and in the weeks and months following the explosion.[15] The American Civil Defense Liaison Committee also reported on the possible effects on a typical city in the United States and concluded that they were especially susceptible to serious damage by blast and fire from an atomic bomb or from a conventional attack with incendiaries. Precise calculations showed that Chicago had 98.3 percent combustible structures, New York 97.7 percent, and San Francisco 99 percent. "What happened in Germany and Japan," the report warned, "could happen here."[16] The American bombing survey also prompted the question "What if the target for a bomb had been an American city?" and concluded that "the overwhelming bulk of the buildings in an American city could not stand up against an atomic bomb bursting a mile or a mile and a half from them."[17]

On the impact of the atomic bombings on the Japanese decision to accept the Potsdam Declaration, the United States Strategic Bombing Survey's report on the atomic bombings, also published in June 1946, was cautious in its conclusions. The evidence from postwar interviews by the Morale Division found that the firebombing campaign was three times as significant as the atomic bombs "in inducing certainty of defeat," while among the Japanese leadership it could not be said "that the atomic bomb convinced the leaders who effected the peace of the necessity of surrender." The report acknowledged that efforts to seek a peace had been pursued for more than a year and were being pursued at the time of Hiroshima. The bomb "considerably speeded up these political maneuverings within the government" but did not cause them.[18] The Soviet view of the significance of the bomb as the instrument that prompted surrender was dismissive. A Soviet diplomat, Nikolaevich Tzekho-nye, had visited Hiroshima two days after the bombing accompanied by a Japanese Foreign Ministry official. His report, including photographs, sent back to Moscow suggested that the damage was the result of just a bigger bomb, less impressive than the firebombing of Tokyo, which he had also witnessed.[19] The Soviet media dismissed the bomb as a significant factor and complained, according to the British ambassador, of a "slander on the Soviet Union's military contribution" in the invasion of Manchuria, which the press insisted was more important in prompting surrender than the bombs—a debate that has continued to the present day. There was no official statement or editorial comment on the effect of the bomb in prompting surrender, a decision that almost certainly rested with Stalin, who remained skeptical of the bomb's military potential.[20]

The imposition of a rigid censorship by the occupation authorities through the Civil Communications Section and the Civil Censorship Detachment left the Japanese population in a state of limbo when it came to interpreting the bombing and understanding its effects. The Allied scientific and medical teams that surveyed the nature of biological damage from the atomic bombs were interested in monitoring the results but were much less concerned with providing practical assistance to the damaged survivors. The medical and scientific teams recorded very precise details of the casualty effects to understand what might happen in future bombing. Groves was given figures calculated by British researchers of the mortality rate at given distances from the "ground zero" explosion, which showed that from 0 to 1,000 feet, 93 percent died, from 1,000 to 2,000 feet, 92 percent, and from 2,000 to 3,000 feet, 86 percent. By 9,000 feet (2.7 kilometers) away from the hypocenter, the figure was almost zero, though that took no account of deaths later from the effects of the initial radiation.[21] Statistics compiled on the effects on women made grim reading. Pregnant women within 3,000 feet who survived all had miscarriages; from 3,000 to 6,500 feet, miscarriages or premature births of infants who mostly died; those in the zone from 6,500 to 10,000 feet had miscarriages and premature births at a level almost five times higher than in peacetime, but otherwise apparently normal infants. Medical researchers found increased incidence of amenorrhea among women and aspermia or low sperm count among men exposed to the bomb up to one kilometer from ground zero.[22]

Japanese researchers had already begun detailed studies of the casualties from radiation in the weeks before the formal surrender, but following an American General Headquarters' decision on September 19, 1945, Japanese researchers were denied the right to undertake independent research or to publish anything on their findings about the medical effects of the two bombs. The Special Manhattan District Engineer Commission did set up a joint program with a cohort of Japanese scientists, but the reports were not made public in Japan until 1953. The Nippon Eiga-sha (Japanese Film Corporation) undertook to make a film of the two bombed cities, but in December 1945 almost all the reels of film were requisitioned by the American authorities. The company was allowed to complete the film, but it was taken to the United States in May 1946 and not allowed to be shown in public. American research on survivors was conducted by the American Atomic Bomb Casualty Commission established in 1947 in Hiroshima and the following year in Nagasaki. The commission carried out examination of those survivors willing to participate, but many resented the intrusion and refused to assist the "vultures [who] carried off the corpses," as one of them put it.[23] The commission's findings were sealed from the Japanese population but exploited in the United States. Only in 1952, after Japanese protests, did the commission begin recommending treatment rather than just cataloguing the conditions they found.[24] The same year, the San Francisco Peace Treaty between the United

States and Japan came into effect, and the occupation ended. Japanese scientists and doctors could at last undertake research freely and independently. When they could report in the 1950s about their research, studies revealed severe psychogenic reactions among survivors shortly after the bombing. A study by the Neuropsychiatric Department at Nagasaki University undertaken during the years of censorship found that survivors suffered not only radiation sickness but also fatigue, apathy, introversion, and hypomnesia (poor recall).[25] Later research also found that Oppenheimer had been wrong: survivors who entered the destroyed zone soon after the explosion suffered from radioactivity still present in soil and structures and from radioactive fallout.[26]

Many of the survivors, known as the *hibakusha* [literally "those who were exposed to the bombs"], discovered there was little interest in their condition when the war ended. Among the wider population, the survivors, many of them deformed or damaged from the ordeal, found themselves shunned as a reminder of the cataclysmic end to the war and were reluctant to speak out about their experience or to be treated as objects of study. Some chose not to reveal that they had been victims, even to their families; others found it difficult to express adequately or at all what they had experienced. In his *Hiroshima Diary*, Hachiya Michihiko, wrote, "What words can we now use, and to what ends. Even: what are words?"[27] Neither did the Japanese government encourage openness, partly from fear that publicity for the sufferers would revive criticism of Japan's war effort and technical backwardness. The 30,000–40,000 Korean survivors—workers and their families in Hiroshima and Nagasaki—were denied the right to medical treatment in Japan. Most of them were sent back to Korea where they found themselves stigmatized rather than assisted. The public view in Korea was ironically to welcome the bombs as the instrument of Korea's liberation from colonial rule, and Korean victims were reduced to silence, like the survivors in Japan. In 1950, one Korean magazine dared to publish an account of "Hiroshima's Last Day" by a writer known only as Student Y, in which the grotesque reality of the raid was made clear along with the alienation experienced by those who survived.[28] When a memorial to the Korean dead in Hiroshima was planned in 1970, the city authorities refused to allow it to be sited in the Hiroshima Peace Memorial Park and repeated the rejection after a further Korean request in 1990. The memorial was built outside the Peace Park but was finally relocated inside the grounds in 1999.[29]

For most Japanese, the years after 1945 were dominated not by memory of the bombing but by the struggle to secure adequate food and the long process of rehabilitation in cities that had been destroyed. The journalist John Morris reported from his journey to Japan in 1946 that every city he visited was a "vast sea of ashes: no bits of walls, no cellars even, just ashes." He accompanied the party when Hirohito visited Yokohama in February 1946. The emperor, who had abandoned his claim to divinity two months before in his New Year's rescript, stood on a surviving rooftop with binoculars to survey the "miles of ashy ruins" without uttering a word.[30] Against Allied expectations, the Japanese population was not driven by hatred for the enemy despite all the fears inspired by presurrender propaganda about the barbarism of the Americans and Australians. A United States Strategic Bombing Survey poll found that only 19 percent of interviewees from Hiroshima and Nagasaki resented the atomic bombings, and nationally only 12 percent, while 35 percent agreed the bombings were Japan's fault.[31] Questionable as the result no doubt was, there was no space for popular protest against the bombing, which was able to develop only much later. In May 1946, the American army journal *Stars and Stripes* even reported that a Nagasaki schoolgirl had been crowned "Miss Atom Bomb."[32] In bombed Tokyo, the returning population lived amidst the ruins, where the black market came to dominate daily life. By October

1945 there were 45,000 open-air stalls, while as many as 17,000 black market rings were identified. For many Japanese, the worse crisis came in 1946, not 1945, when the daily ration was reduced to just 1,050 calories for the urban population. Food consumption was 59 percent of the prewar level, and starvation was avoided only by an American decision, made reluctantly, to release additional food stocks across the summer of 1946.[33] In these circumstances, official neglect of those who had survived the bombing can more readily be comprehended.

THE YEARS OF SILENCE ended in 1952 when Japanese sovereignty was fully restored. Before then, the American occupation authority had begun to allow some publications that addressed the bombing. The classic study of Hiroshima by John Hersey was translated in 1949. That same year, the occupiers allowed Nagai Takashi, a Catholic doctor, to publish *Bells of Nagasaki* so long as he also included a section describing Japanese military atrocities in Manila (a decision that had the unintended effect of equating the two narratives as equally atrocious). Nagai died in 1951 of the effects of radiation, but he was approved by the Americans because of his argument that the dead at Nagasaki were a sacrifice of divine grace to atone for the war rather than the victims of an indiscriminate weapon of mass destruction.[34] The book proposed by the young Masako Taorezu, fifteen when the bomb dropped on Nagasaki, which contained harrowing descriptions of the dead and dying, was rejected by the American censors as a threat to "public tranquillity" because it implied that the bombing was "a crime against humanity." Her slim volume was finally published in the city in 1949.[35] The ending of the Allied censorship regime in 1952 at last allowed public discussion of the bombing and the dissemination of hard information about what had happened. The first photographs allowed in Japan of the results of the bombing were published in the illustrated paper *Asahi Gurafu* in August 1952. The issue sold out on the first day, and 520,000 copies were eventually printed. The same month, fifteen survivors founded the Atomic Bomb Survivors' Society in Hiroshima, the first permitted organization to represent the *hibakusha*. A second society was founded in Nagasaki two years later.[36]

The government response in Japan was to avoid privileging the survivors of the bombing in order to take advantage of the United States' role in reconstruction and the promise of security in the face of Soviet and, from 1949, Chinese communism. In the San Francisco Peace Treaty that formally ended the war on April 28, 1952, the Japanese government agreed to a clause that there would be no claims for reparation for the damage caused by the bombing. The Treaty of Mutual Cooperation and Security between the United States and Japan that came into effect the same day also inhibited any questioning of the bombing, while at the same time the government could use the agreement to avoid discussion of Japanese war responsibility and the atrocities and repression that went with it. At home, the claim for compensation by bomb victims from both atomic and firebombing attacks was refused in case it encouraged similar claims by those who had suffered under Japanese imperial control.[37] The law passed in February 1942 promising that the state would repay the damage caused to homes by bombing and compensate the injured was overturned in 1946, leaving the millions who had lost their homes to find their own means for re-housing. The measures for provision of relief for wartime casualties were terminated in October 1945 so that medical assistance had to be found at the victims' own expense. Only in 1980 did the survivors begin legal proceedings against the government, but compensation was again refused on the argument that in the struggle for the nation's existence, sacrifices had to be shared equally across Japanese society.[38]

From the 1950s onward, the *hibakusha* began to organize collectively not only to campaign for better welfare provision and medical assistance but also to inaugurate a peace movement specifically directed at the abolition of nuclear weapons. In August 1954, a national council was established representing the survivors. A year later, a World Conference Against Atomic and Hydrogen Bombs was hosted in Hiroshima, which has met every year since 1955. The various autonomous groups involved joined together in 1956 into the Confederation of A-Bomb and H-Bomb Sufferers Organizations [*Hidankyo*]. The mayors of Hiroshima and Nagasaki gave annual speeches on the need for peace and an end to nuclear weapons and finally in 1975 agreed to a joint "Hiroshima-Nagasaki Partnership for Peace." In 1985 they were instrumental in establishing the World Conference of Mayors for Peace through Intercity Solidarity, which by the 1989 conference had attracted 130 cities from 30 countries.[39] The *Hidankyo* federation succeeded in winning concessions on health care and welfare at home, beginning with legislation in March 1957, while it also set out to establish a broader antinuclear network abroad. An "Appeal from Hiroshima and Nagasaki for a Total Ban and Elimination of Nuclear Weapons," begun in 1985, spread to 160 countries by 1994 and generated 100 million signatures. The same year, the Japanese Diet finally passed a law compensating victims and their families with a payment of 100,000 yen each. Simultaneously, public attitudes toward the United States hardened, encouraged by American bombing in Vietnam with the wide use of napalm incendiaries, which seemed to repeat the suffering inflicted on civilians in Japan. A survey in 1970 found that 38 percent of respondents resented the American decision to drop the bombs, while only 19 percent now blamed the Japanese military and political leadership.[40]

The international focus on the antinuclear campaign largely ignored the victims of the firebombing. The fate of Tokyo was marginalized in accounts of the war both in Japan and abroad. The city instead contributed to the atomic bomb debate, and in 1963 the Tokyo District Court passed a ruling that the atomic bombs "violated fundamental codes of war," though no legal case was allowed to go through the courts.[41] Between 1948 and 1950, the American occupation authority suggested that the Tokyo City Council exhume and cremate thousands of victims from the firebombing. Some 450 urns of their cremated remains were placed in the memorial to the earthquake victims of 1923 rather than in a memorial dedicated to the bombing. Thereafter, the Tokyo municipal government made no effort to memorialize the bombing. Only in the late 1960s did the firebombing resurface as an element in the city's public history thanks to the support of the socialist governor of the capital, Minobe Ryōkichi. In 1970, a Society to Record the Tokyo Air Raids was founded, and in 1973 it published a full account in the Great Tokyo Air Raid War Damage Documentation using the recollections of survivors; forty other Japanese cities did the same.[42] Plans to build a Tokyo Peace Museum, which would record the conventional bombing rather than just the atomic bombs, were first mooted in the 1970s but provoked a long debate over what the museum should or should not say about the Japanese war effort. In the end, the municipal government rejected the idea and replaced it with a monument to the Tokyo war dead, which was opened in the Yokoami Park in March 2001. In 2007–2008, a lawsuit for compensation was finally filed against the Japanese government but without success.[43]

The problems faced in creating a museum to the bomb victims in Tokyo was replicated elsewhere when in the 1990s more cities began to plan museums to record the incendiary bombing that they had experienced. The Osaka International Peace Center, opened in the 1990s, was designed to record the experience of Osakans from some fifty air raids during the war but also to set that experience in the context of Japanese treatment of the Asians they conquered. In 1996, conservative lobby groups challenged the historical representation of Japan's war effort in the museum in Osaka and forced the curators to remove reference to Japan's harsh imperial rule. Other peace museums found themselves subject to similar pressure if they tried to marry Japanese suffering under the bombs with the wider reasons for why the war was fought, and with what consequences for those conquered. The result has been a division in Japan between memories of the bombing as a direct consequence of Japan's disastrous war of aggression and memories of Japanese victimization in a war fought to free Asia from Western imperialism.[44]

THE VIEW FROM THE United States on the bombing, which has focused almost entirely on the atomic bombs, took a different direction. Although some prominent wartime leaders suggested after the war that the bombs had been unnecessary and unlawful—most famously the supreme commander of the Allied forces in Europe, Gen. Dwight Eisenhower, and the presidential adviser Adm. William Leahy—the overwhelming majority of Americans supported the decision. In response to such criticism as there was, the standard narrative of military necessity was defined by Henry Stimson in an article written for *Harper's Magazine* in 1947, which has been widely referenced ever since. "My chief purpose," wrote Stimson, "was to end the war in victory with the least cost in the lives of the men in the armies I had helped to raise." Use of the bomb, he claimed, was "our least abhorrent choice." He hoped that his statement would influence a future generation of "educators and historians."[45]

Public sentiment broadly approved the necessity of using the bombs. In September 1945, when the National Opinion Research

Center at the University of Chicago asked a cohort of respondents what they would have done if confronted with the decision Truman faced, only 4 percent replied that they would not have dropped the bombs. In the decades that followed, the proportion of those in favor of the operation remained around two-thirds of respondents, although with a rising proportion of the sample expressing opposition to the bombing. A 1982 Harris poll found 63 percent in favor, 26 percent against, but by then there was a significant generational difference. A Gallup survey in 2005 found that 70 percent of those aged over 65 favored the bombing, but among those between 18 and 29, only 47 percent.[46] The official narrative of the bombs and their purpose has nevertheless remained, although it is far from being unanimous. There are small annual peace ceremonies in the United States that memorialize the victims of the Hiroshima and Nagasaki bombings, including the Annual Interfaith Peace Gathering in New York, founded in 1994 by a Japanese Buddhist monk; the San Francisco Bay Area Peace Lantern Ceremony begun in 2002; and at the small town of Ashland in Oregon, the annual Hiroshima-Nagasaki Vigil. But these are marginal events linked to the broader nuclear disarmament movement, unlikely to disturb very greatly the established narrative.[47] On the conventional firebombing there is by contrast little public debate or memorialization.

The gulf that separates United States and Japanese responses to the wartime bombing was brought into sharp relief in the 1990s over a decision by the Smithsonian National Air and Space Museum in Washington, D.C., to hold an exhibition on the fiftieth anniversary of the atomic bombings centered around the surviving *Enola Gay*, the B-29 that dropped the uranium bomb on Hiroshima. The museum began planning the exhibition in 1993, but when the first version of the script was released, including images and text on the Japanese victims of the bombing, there was vigorous protest from veteran groups including the Air Force Association and the American Legion. They saw the exhibition as an attempt to undermine the heroic narrative of the *Enola Gay*'s operation and to desecrate the collective memory of the sacrifices made by American service personnel in the Second World War. The exhibition had forty-nine images of Japanese victims, but only three of Americans.[48] It also carried the caption, regarded as provocative, that "to this day, controversy has raged about whether dropping this weapon [the atomic bomb] on Japan was necessary to end the war quickly"—a claim that critics regarded as axiomatic rather than open to question.[49] The controversy was taken up in Congress when Senator Nancy Kassebaum of Kansas introduced Senate Resolution 257 to warn the museum not to impugn "the memory of those who gave their lives for freedom."[50] The wave of protest did not lead to cancellation, as many critics wanted, but the museum excised the sections on Japanese victims, reworded the offending texts, and opened the exhibition on June 28, 1995. The *Enola Gay* is now exhibited at the Udvar-Hazy Center of the Air and Space Museum in Chantilly, Virginia, accompanied by a text simply stating that B-29s "dropped a single bomb on Hiroshima and Nagasaki. Japan surrendered days later." A model of the aircraft in the museum shop carries the legend "this World War II bomber brought an end to the war on the Pacific front," reinforcing the standard narrative that the atomic bombs provoked surrender.[51]

Japanese critics saw the result of the museum controversy as an effort to silence the broader message of the *hibakusha* about the necessity for peace and nuclear disarmament. The Japanese organizations did succeed in preventing the U.S. Postal Service from issuing a stamp to mark the fiftieth anniversary with the caption under the aircraft, "Atomic bombs hasten war's end, 1945."[52] While the controversy unfolded, the UN General Assembly in December 1994 hosted a debate prompted by the World Health Organization on the question whether nuclear bombing was against international law (in which the Japanese representative abstained). The assembly resolved to ask the International Court of Justice to give a ruling on the question. The court was inundated with more than 3 million Japanese "declarations of public conscience" against the use of nuclear weapons, while the mayor of Hiroshima, Takashi Hiraoka, was a key witness. The final ruling in 1996 declared that the use of nuclear weapons would not necessarily be unlawful depending on circumstances and so long as the use or threat of nuclear weapons complied with broader principles of customary international and humanitarian law.[53] In July 2007, an International People's Tribunal on the Dropping of the Bombs established in Hiroshima ruled that the bombing constituted a crime against humanity, but the tribunal has no jurisdiction.[54] There was not, and still is not, an instrument in international law that proscribes the use of nuclear weapons.

THE QUESTION RAISED AT the United Nations in 1994 was an indication of the popular awareness of the issues surrounding bombing and its legal restriction. The legitimacy or otherwise of the use of nuclear weapons in 1945, or indeed of the area bombing of cities in Europe and Japan, does not alter the fact of their use, but it has become a current concern over why and with what legal justification bombing was conducted in the past. Truman in August 1945, as he recalled in his memoirs, was concerned that the bomb on Hiroshima "would be used as a weapon of war in the manner prescribed by the laws of war," and his regular insistence that the city was "only a military base" underlined his belief that the laws of war were not violated.[55] On the firebombing of Tokyo and other cities there was much less concern, although Stimson in the summer of 1945 worried that area bombing should not "have the United States get the reputation of outdoing Hitler in atrocities."[56] Here, too, insistence by Arnold that the bombing was a strategic necessity because of the dispersed nature of the urban military targets gave the campaign a legal gloss. Ethical concerns did not worry LeMay. In his memoirs he wrote about Tokyo: "We knew we were going to kill a lot of women and kids when we bombed that town. Had to be done."[37] Nor did any ethical concerns limit what the postwar U.S. Air Force went on to do in the area bombing of North Korea during the Korean War, or in the bombing and defoliation carried out in the Vietnam War, both campaigns that replicated the belief that saturation bombing would yield results as it had in 1945. Nor did they have any effect on the nuclear arms race and the stockpiling of warheads despite the hope, expressed by Oppenheimer and others, that the experience of seeing one atomic explosion would be enough to encourage a warless world.

Since 1945, there have been contested interpretations of the bombing as consistent with or a violation of international law and the prevailing laws and customs of armed conflict. That there can be any argument at all that killing 300,000 civilians in three hours of night bombing and two nuclear strikes is lawful has relied on the ambiguous wording and broad interpretation of the chief instruments designed to regulate the conduct of war. The Hague Conventions of 1899 and 1907 specified that the "means of injury to the enemy is not unlimited"; Convention IV in 1907 specifically proscribed attacks on civilians or civilian property through aerial bombardment. The advent of aerial warfare in the First World War, which generally ignored the convention, encouraged the major powers to define more clearly what was and was not permissible in selecting targets for attack. A decision was made at the Washington Conference in 1921–1922 to establish a committee of jurists to draw up regulations governing air war. The resulting Hague Rules for Air Warfare, published in 1923, made civilian immunity a central principle. Article 22 outlawed any bombing aimed to deliberately destroy civilian property or to kill noncombatants; article

24 limited bombing only to clearly identifiable military objectives and within the "immediate vicinity of the operation of the land forces."[38] Although the Hague Rules were not formally ratified by any of the major states, they were treated as if they had the force of international law.

These proscriptions proved open to interpretation. There was conflicting opinion over whether noncombatants also included war workers in military industry or those workers in communications and utility industries whose work helped sustain the war effort. There was also the problem that civilian immunity was a priority in "undefended towns," but perhaps not in towns with antiaircraft defenses and a military garrison, an argument later used by Japan to justify its bombing of the Chinese capital of Chongqing in 1939–1940. In both Britain and the United States, there was an understanding that civilians ought to be protected against deliberate or negligent attack, and this view was reinforced by strong criticism in the West against Italian bombing in Ethiopia, Japanese bombing in China, and German bombing during the Spanish Civil War. In late 1937, the U.S. State Department stated that "any general bombing of an extensive area wherein resides a large population engaged in peaceful pursuits is unwarranted and contrary to the principles of law and humanity."[39]

In Britain, the government and the chiefs of staff both reiterated the Hague Rules in 1939 on the eve of war. The deliberate bombing of civilians was illegal; only legitimate military targets could be attacked, but not if the attack would involve negligent harm to civilians. The Air Ministry added that bombing through cloud or at night would also be illegal. An interdepartmental committee set up in August concluded "it is clearly illegal to bombard a populated area in the hope of hitting a legitimate target."[60] Winston Churchill in January 1940 considered indiscriminate bombing as a "new and odious form of warfare" (although this did not prevent him from hoping in June for an "absolutely devastating, extermi-nating attack . . . on the Nazi homeland").[61] American air force doc-trine on the eve of the Pacific war was based on a bombing policy of precise hits on military targets rather than urban areas. President Roosevelt in his appeal to the potential belligerents on September 1, 1939, added his weight to the argument that bombing which killed civilians had "profoundly shocked the conscience of humanity." Killing civilians or bombing unfortified towns was, he continued, "inhuman barbarism."[62]

In both cases, military necessity was used as an argument for switching from limited bombing of military targets to the deliber-ate bombing of city centers and the civilian populations that inhab-ited them. Enemy cities could be dressed up in abstract language about "industrial centers," while the assertion became normalized that war workers were a legitimate target who could be "de-housed" rather than deliberately killed and injured, which is what the strat-egy amounted to. In the international law of war, there was also a poorly defined right of reciprocal retaliation against an enemy who violated the laws of war, although retaliation was supposed to be proportionate and to indicate some military advantage. In Brit-ain, Churchill argued in cabinet meetings in May 1940 for bomb-ing German industry and risking the death of civilians through "unrestricted air warfare" because German military behavior in the invasion of Poland gave "ample justification" for retaliation. Tru-man argued a similar case for waging total air war against Japan because Japanese forces "have abandoned all pretense of obeying international laws of warfare," which permitted reciprocal retali-ation against "the enemy individuals and property."[63] It is evident that the destruction of Tokyo and the atomic bombings evaded the principle of proportionality and the protection expected for civilian populations from the Hague Conventions onward, whatever way "retaliation" or "reciprocity" is defined.[64] The argument often used since, that Japanese atrocities and the mistreatment of people under imperial rule justified the bombings, overlooks the fact that these abuses were treated as war crimes by the Allies, and Japanese military and political leaders, as well as commanders in the field, were expected to pay the price for their violations. Significantly, the mass killing of civilians from the air was not part of the indictment in the Tokyo Military Tribunal nor in the Nuremberg Trials, because British and American air forces had done exactly that, and deliberately, in the last years of war, abandoning the restrictions on targeting civilians in force when the war began.

In the decades after 1945, some effort was made to rein in the effects of indiscriminate bombing, first in the Geneva Conventions of 1949 (which advocated the creation of sanctuaries for vulnerable civilians) then more explicitly in the Geneva Additional Protocol of 1977. This prescribed more comprehensive protection from bombing for civilian populations (articles 48, 51 [2] and 51 [4]). These limitations were repeated in the Rome Statute, which established the International Criminal Court.[65] In the provisions of the Additional Protocol, the bombing of Tokyo, Hiroshima, and Nagasaki would now be considered war crimes. Both Britain and the United States argued against including nuclear weapons in the 1977 protocol, so that their use would not necessarily constitute a violation of international law. Earlier American military plans for a nuclear strike against Soviet targets had continued to ignore any effort to limit damage to an enemy population. The Joint Chiefs of Staff in October 1945 had argued that future atomic bombs should be used against "centers of population with a view to forcing an enemy state to yield through terror and disintegration of national morale."[66] British planning similarly emphasized the destruction through nuclear bombardment of the enemy population as much as the military capacity of the Soviet enemy. A cabinet committee set up in 1960 to evaluate how to kill a (Soviet) city with nuclear warfare concluded that "people were the scale to be used in assessing the effects of damage."[67]

Not until the late twentieth and the twenty-first centuries has military thinking shifted unequivocally in the West against the idea of deliberately targeting civilians. In the United States, the Department of Defense in 2016 finally spelled out that attacking a civilian population to undermine morale was no longer legally acceptable, while bombing the center of a city was "patently" and "manifestly" illegal.[68] At the United Nations, a Treaty on the Prohibition of Nuclear Weapons was introduced in July 2017, with effect from January 2021, and was signed by 122 countries—though neither Japan nor the United States joined the signatories. None of these efforts to define more clearly in the international laws of war the limits of targeting from the air have been effective in conflicts from Korea to the recent wars in Ukraine and Gaza, nor would they prevent a future nuclear war. The conclusion from the bombing of Japan in 1945 is not to understand whether it was necessary or not but why it was thought to be necessary at the time. Understanding the reasons for the incremental radicalization of strategy in 1945, and for the elaboration of a relative morality to legitimize the prosecution of ruthless total war, ought surely to be an important contribution to avoiding its repetition.

Acknowledgments

I HAVE SEVERAL PEOPLE TO THANK FOR ADVICE IN PREPARING THE manuscript or reading some of it: Rana Mitter, Aaron Moore, and Phillips O'Brien. I would particularly like to thank Richard Hammond, who supplied me with some of the material from the Truman Library collection while there for his own research. I would also like to acknowledge the help and support from my two editors, Simon Winder in London and Steve Forman in New York, and the contribution of my agent, Cara Jones. The team at Norton helped to get the book into shape and prepare it for sale. Many thanks to Don Rifkin, Steve Attardo, Lauren Abbate, Gina Savoy, and Steven Pace, and to the cartographer, Mapping Specialists, Ltd., for executing the useful overview maps in the front matter. I would also like to thank Matthew Hutchinson, Olivia Kumar, and Eva Hodgkin from Penguin, who look after publicity and sales at the British end.

Notes

PREFACE: "IT WILL BE ALL-OUT"

1. Larry Bland, ed., *The Papers of George Catlett Marshall: Volume 2: "We Cannot Delay," July 1, 1939–December 6 1941* (Baltimore: Johns Hopkins University Press, 1986), 678, memorandum from Robert Sherwood to David Hulburd, "General Marshall's conference today," November 15, 1941.

2. The National Archives, Kew, London, HO 338/7, Report of the British Mission to Japan, "The Bombing of Japan," October 18, 1946, 7.

3. Curtis LeMay with MacKinlay Kantor, *Mission with LeMay: My Story* (New York: Doubleday, 1965), 383.

4. Ferenc Szasz, *British Scientists and the Manhattan Project: The Los Alamos Years* (London: Macmillan, 1992), xiii–xix.

CHAPTER 1: DEFEAT OF JAPAN

1. Edward Miller, *War Plan Orange: The U. S. Strategy to Defeat Japan 1897–1945* (Annapolis, MD: Naval Institute Press, 1991), p. 150.

2. Miller, *War Plan Orange*, 153–54, 156.

3. Stephen Morewood, *The British Defence of Egypt 1935–1940* (London: Frank Cass, 2005), 181–84; David Horner, "Australia in 1942: A Pivotal Year," in *Australia 1942: In the Shadow of War*, ed. Peter Dean (Cambridge: Cambridge University Press, 2013), 12–15; Davide Borsani, "The Rising Challenge in the Asia-Pacific: Britain and Imperial Defence in the Age of the Ten-Year Rule, 1919–1932," *Quaderni di Scienze Politiche* 23 (2023): 88, 93–96; Richard Dunley, "Rebuilding the Mills of Sea Power: Interwar British Planning for Economic Warfare Against Japan," *International History Review* 44, no. 5 (2022): 1093–96, 1102–3.

4. Charles Burgess, "Pacific Fleet to Singapore? Deterrence,

Warfighting, and Anglo-American Plans for the Defense of Southeast Asia, 1937–1941," *Diplomacy and Statecraft* 34, no. 2 (2023): 258–61, 267–74.

5. R. Futrell, *Ideas, Concepts, Doctrine: A History of Basic Thinking in the United States Air Force* (Maxwell, AL: Air University Press, 1971), 28.

6. National Archives and Records Administration (hereafter NARA), RG165/888.96, memorandum Army War Plans Division, "Aviation versus Coast Fortification," December 6, 1935, 5.

7. NARA, RG94/452, memorandum for Chief of Staff, "Review of Present Approved Airplane Program," July 19, 1938; R. Krauskopf, "The Army and the Strategic Bomber, 1930–1939: Part II," *Military Affairs* 22 (1958–59): 212–13.

8. Library of Congress (hereafter LC), Mitchell Papers, Box 27, papers "Aviation in the Next War" and "Give America Airplanes," n.d.

9. LC, Andrews Papers, Box 9, lecture on "The GHQ Air Force," March 26, 1935, and memorandum "the GHQ Air Force," n.d.

10. United States Air Force Academy, McDonald Papers, Ser. V, Box 8, Folder 8, "Development of the U.S. Air Forces' Philosophy of Air Warfare Prior to Our Entry into World War II"; LC, Andrews Papers, Box 11, Maj. Harold George, "An Inquiry into the Subject War."

11. Kenneth Werrell, *Blankets of Fire: U.S. Bombers over Japan During World War II* (Washington, DC: Smithsonian Institution Press, 1996), 39–40.

12. NARA, RG 94/452.1, memorandum for the Army Chief of Staff, "Airplane Replacement and Development Program," September 21, 1939; RG 94/580, memorandum for the Army Chief of Staff from Gen. George Strong, May 10, 1940.

13. NARA, RG 165/888, memorandum by Marshall for the President, October 10, 1939.

14. Miller, *War Plan Orange*, 156.

15. Conrad Crane, *American Airpower Strategy in World War II: Bombs, Cities, Civilians, and Oil* (Lawrence: University Press of Kansas, 2016), 167–68.

16. Edward Young, *Building Engines for War: Air-Cooled Radial Engine*

Production in Britain and America in World War II (Warrendale, PA: SAE International, 2024), 255–57.

17. Rudolf Janssens, *"What Future for Japan?": U.S. Wartime Planning for the Postwar Era 1942–1945* (Amsterdam: University of Amsterdam, 1995), 166.

18. On islands, see Alvin Coox, "Strategic Bombing in the Pacific 1942–1945," in *Case Studies in Strategic Bombardment*, ed. R. Cargill Hall (Washington, DC: Air Force History Program, 1998), 263; on bats, see Janssens, *"What Future for Japan?,"* 49–50.

19. Ray Monk, *Inside the Centre: The Life of J. Robert Oppenheimer* (London: Jonathan Cape, 2012), 306–9; William Miscamble, *The Most Controversial Decision: Truman, the Atom Bomb, and the Defeat of Japan* (Cambridge: Cambridge University Press, 2011), 7–11.

20. NARA, RG165/55, Roosevelt to Marshall, March 8, 1943.

21. NARA, RG165/55, Marshall memorandum for the JCS, "Operations in Burma, March 1943."

22. Haywood Hansell, *The Strategic Air War Against Germany and Japan* (Washington, DC: Office of Air Force History, 1986), 142.

23. The National Archives, Kew, London (hereafter TNA), AIR 20/1590, Roosevelt to Churchill, November 11, 1943; Mountbatten to the British Chiefs of Staff, November 20, 1943.

24. Hansell, *Strategic Air War*, 139–41; Werell, *Blankets of Fire*, 50–51.

25. TNA, WO 193/604, Joint Staff Mission, Washington, DC, to War Office, March 7, 1944; Daniel Schwabe, *Burning Japan: Air Force Bombing Strategy Change in the Pacific* (Lincoln, NE: Potomac Books, 2015), 54–56.

26. TNA, WO 193/604, Air Ministry to Southeast Asia Command, January 6, 1944; Chiefs of Staff to British Air Mission, Washington, DC, May 18, 1944.

27. Hansell, *Strategic Air War*, 144–46; Coox, "Strategic Bombing in the Pacific," 274–80; Schwabe, *Burning Japan*, 21–22.

28. Coox, "Strategic Bombing in the Pacific," 278–80.

29. TNA, AIR 20/1590 Note by Joint Planning Staff, March 25, 1944; War Cabinet, Joint Planning Staff memorandum, March 17, 1944.

30. Details from Coox, "Strategic Bombing in the Pacific," 280–83.

31. Werrell, *Blankets of Fire*, 256–57.

32. Warren Kozak, *LeMay: The Life and Wars of General Curtis LeMay* (Washington, DC: Regnery, 2009), 181.

33. Curtis LeMay with MacKinlay Kantor, *Mission with LeMay: My Story* (New York: Doubleday, 1965), 322.

34. LC, LeMay Papers, Box 11, Lemay to Chief of Staff Lauris Norstad, September 12, 1944, 1–2.

35. Coox, "Strategic Bombing in the Pacific," pp. 289–91.

CHAPTER 2: AMERICAN "AREA BOMBING"

1. Library of Congress (hereafter LC), LeMay Papers, Box 11, Norstad to LeMay, April 18, 1945.

2. LC, LeMay Papers, Box 11, Arnold to LeMay, March 21, 1945.

3. Truman Library, Atomic Bomb Collection, Box 1, "Military Use of the Atomic Bomb," report based on records of the Operational Plans Division, 31.

4. Details all from Haywood Hansell, *The Strategic Air War Against Germany and Japan* (Washington, DC: Office of Air Force History, 1986), 166–67, 174.

5. United States Air Force Academy (hereafter USAFA), Hansell Papers, Ser. I, Box I, Arnold to Hansell, September 22, 1944.

6. David Fedman and Cary Karacas, "A Cartographic Fade to Black: Mapping the Destruction of Urban Japan During World War II," *Journal of Historical Geography* 38, no. 3 (2012): 308–11.

7. Alvin Coox, "Strategic Bombing in the Pacific 1942–1945," in *Case Studies in Strategic Bombardment*, ed. R. Cargill Hall (Washington, DC: Air Force History Program, 1998), 296–97.

8. USAFA, Hansell Papers, Ser. I, Box 1, Hansell to Arnold, December 16, 1944.

9. Daniel Schwabe, *Burning Japan: Air Force Bombing Strategy Change in the Pacific* (Lincoln, NE: Potomac Books, 2015), 109.

10. Warren Kozak, *LeMay: The Life and Wars of General Curtis LeMay* (Washington, DC: Regnery, 2009), 200–201.

11. LC, LeMay Papers, Box 38, "Statistical Control Unit: XXI Bomber Command: Graphic Summary of Operations, March 1, 1945," 15.

12. LC, LeMay Papers, Box 38, "Statistical Control Unit," 2, 6, 11–12.

13. Curtis LeMay with MacKinley Kantor, *Mission with LeMay: My Story* (New York: Doubleday, 1965), 355.

14. Fedman and Karacas, "Cartographic Fade to Black," 309.

15. Richard Overy, *The Bombing War: Europe 1939–1945* (London: Allen Lane, 2013), 328–31.

16. LC, Arnold Papers, Reel 199, Arnold to Maj. General Echols, April 26, 1943.

17. W. Hays Park, "'Precision' and 'Area' Bombing: Who Did Which, and When?," *Journal of Strategic Studies* 18, no. 1 (1995): 153–56, 162–64. In the last four months of 1944, 76 percent of the bombing was nonvisual and used radar.

18. The National Archives, Kew, London (hereafter TNA), AIR 52/93, National Defense Research Committee, "Report on Theory and Tactics of Incendiary Bombing," October 9, 1942, 3–4, 11.

19. Schwabe, *Burning Japan*, 48–49.

20. Fedman and Karacas, "Cartographic Fade to Black," 312–13.

21. TNA, AIR 14/1813, Incendiary Panel: "General Analysis of Japanese Urban Areas," US Joint Target Group, February 28, 1945. On British zoning practice, see Richard Overy, "The 'Weak Link'? The Perception of the German Working Class by RAF Bomber Command, 1940–1945," *Labour History Review* 77, no. 1 (2012): 26. British zones were 1, 2(a), 2(b), 3, 4, and 5, from heavily built-up residential (1) to industrial zone (5). Zones 1 and 2(a) were priority areas, zone 5 not regarded as especially profitable.

22. Dylan Plung, "The Japanese Village at Dugway Proving Ground: An Unexamined Context to the Firebombing of Japan," *Asia-Pacific Journal: Japan Focus* 16, no. 8 (2018): 5–9; Marine Guillaume, "Napalm in US Bombing Doctrine and Practice, 1942–1975," *Asia-Pacific Journal: Japan Focus* 14, no. 23 (2016): 1–3; Malcolm Gladwell, *The Bomber Mafia* (New York: Little, Brown, 2021): 153–56, 159–60; Fedman and Karacas,

"Cartographic Fade to Black," 313–14; TNA, AIR 14/1813, Joint Target Group report, 2.

23. TNA, DSIR 4/2848, Preliminary Summary Report, IEP memorandum no. 2, "Wood Moisture Conditions to Be Expected in Occupied Japanese Houses in Summer," Edgewood Arsenal, MD; IEP "Report of British-American Subcommittee on Construction of Incendiary Test Room Simulating Interior of Japanese Dwelling House," February 26, 1945.

24. Schwabe, *Burning Japan*, 52–53.

25. Fedman and Karacas, "Cartographic Fade to Black," 318; Schwabe, *Burning Japan*, 69.

26. Conrad Crane, *American Airpower Strategy in World War II: Bombs, Cities, Civilians, and Oil* (Lawrence: University Press of Kansas, 2016), 169.

27. Coox, "Strategic Bombing in the Pacific," 313–15; Kenneth Werrell, *Blankets of Fire: U. S. Bombers over Japan During World War II* (Washington, DC: Smithsonian Press, 1996), 142, 147.

28. LeMay and Kantor, *Mission with LeMay*, 347.

29. Schwabe, *Burning Japan*, 113; Charles Webster and Noble Frankland, *The Strategic Air Offensive Against Germany*, vol. 4 (London: HMSO, 1961), 143–48.

30. Kozak, *LeMay*, 218.

31. Thomas Earle, " 'It Made a Lot of Sense to Kill Skilled Workers': The Firebombing of Tokyo in March 1945," *Journal of Military History* 66, no. 1 (2002): 121.

32. Masahiko Yamabe, "Thinking Now About the Great Tokyo Air Raid," *Asia-Pacific Journal: Japan Focus* 9, no. 3 (2011): 3; Ichikawa Hiroo, "Reconstructing Tokyo: The Attempt to Transform the Metropolis," in *Rebuilding Urban Japan After 1945*, ed. Carola Hein, Jeffry Diefendorf, and Ishida Yorifusa (Basingstoke, UK: Palgrave/Macmillan, 2003), 50–51.

33. LC, LeMay Papers, Box 37, HQ XX Bomber Command, "Enemy Anti-Aircraft Defense Bulletin," January 1, 1945.

34. Ishida Yorifusa, "Japanese Cities and Planning in the Reconstruction

Period: 1945–55," in *Rebuilding Urban Japan After 1945*, ed. Carola Hein, Jeffry Diefendorf, and Ishida Yorifusapp (Basingstoke, UK: Palgrave/Macmillan, 2003), 17–18.

35. Coox, "Strategic Bombing in the Pacific," 271–72.

36. Gennifer Weisenfeld, *Gas Mask Nation: Visualizing Civil Air Defense in Wartime Japan* (Chicago: University of Chicago Press, 2023), 54–56, 79–80.

37. Civil Defense Liaison Office, "Fire Effects of Bombing Attacks," National Security Resources Board, August 1951, 18–19; U.S. Strategic Bombing Survey (hereafter USSBS), Pacific Theater, Report 11, "Final Report Covering Air Raid Protection," February 1947, 6, 69, 200.

38. Thomas Havens, *Valley of Darkness: The Japanese People and World War II* (New York: Norton, 1978), 161–62.

39. Dylan Plung, "The Impact of Urban Evacuation in Japan During World War II," *Asia-Pacific Journal: Japan Focus* 19, no. 1 (2021): 1–3; Havens, *Valley of Darkness*, 169–70.

40. Civil Defense Liaison Office, "Fire Effects of Bombing Attacks," 13–14; Robert Nathaus, "Making the Fires That Beat Japan," in *Fire and the Air War*, ed. Horatio Bond (Boston, MA: National Fire Protection Association, 1946), 147–48.

41. Bret Fisk, "The Tokyo Air Raids in the Words of Those Who Survived," *Asia-Pacific Journal: Japan Focus* 9, no. 3 (2011): 2–6.

42. Robert Guillain, *I Saw Tokyo Burning: An Eyewitness Narrative from Pearl Harbor to Hiroshima* (New York: Doubleday, 1981), 185–87.

43. Yamabe, "Thinking Now About the Great Tokyo Air Raid," 4. This is the statistic used in the Tokyo Memorial Hall to the victims.

44. Coox, "Strategic Bombing in the Pacific," 319.

45. Steven Casey, *The War Beat, Pacific: The American Media at War Against Japan* (Oxford: Oxford University Press, 2021), 278.

46. Werrell, *Blankets of Fire*, 162.

47. LC, LeMay Papers, Box 11, Arnold to LeMay, March 21, 1945.

48. LC, LeMay Papers, Box 11, Norstad to LeMay, April 3, 1945.

49. LeMay and Kantor, *Mission with LeMay*, 373.

50. Richard Overy, ed., *The New York Times Complete World War II* (New York: Black Dog & Leventhal, 2013), 508, edition of March 11, 1945.

51. LC, LeMay Papers, Box 16, Air Intelligence Report, vol. 1, no. 2, March 15, 1945; Kozak, *LeMay*, 232–33.

52. Casey, *War Beat, Pacific*, 279.

53. David Earhart, *Certain Victory: Images of World War II in the Japanese Media* (New York: Routledge, 2008), 445–48.

54. Noriko Kawamura, *Emperor Hirohito and the Pacific War* (Seattle: University of Washington Press, 2015), 147–49.

55. LC, LeMay Papers, Box 37, XX Air Force, "Operations Cumulative Through 14 August 1945," 1; USSBS, Pacific Theater, Report 11, 2, 9–11; TNA, AIR 48/68, USSBS Report "The Strategic Air Operation of Very Heavy Bombardment in the War Against Japan: Final Report," September 1, 1946, Appendix A.

56. LC, LeMay Papers, Box 11, Norstad to LeMay, September 23, 1944; Arnold to LeMay, December 17, 1944.

57. USAFA, Hansell Papers, Ser. I, Box I, Arnold to Hansell, December 30, 1944.

58. Truman Library, Atomic Bomb Collection, Box 1, OPD report "Military Use of the Atomic Bomb," 31; William Ralph, "Improvised Destruction: Arnold, LeMay, and the Firebombing of Japan," *War in History* 13, no. 4 (2006): 516.

59. John Huston, ed., *American Air Power Comes of Age: General Henry "Hap" Arnold's World War II Diaries: Volume 2* (Maxwell, AL: Air University Press, 2002), 326, 330, entries for June 13 and 15, 1945.

60. Gian Gentile, "Shaping the Past Battlefield 'For the Future': The United States Strategic Bombing Survey's Evaluation of the American Air War Against Japan," *Journal of Military History* 64, no. 4 (2000): 1107–12.

61. LeMay and Kantor, *Mission with LeMay*, 387.

62. Crane, *American Airpower Strategy*, 162.

63. Huston, *American Air Power Comes of Age*, 314, 322, diary entry for June 16, 1945.

64. Casey, *War Beat Pacific*, 270–71; John Dower, *Cultures of War: Pearl Harbor, Hiroshima, 9–11, Iraq* (New York: Norton, 2010), 183–84.

65. Barton Bernstein, "Eclipsed by Hiroshima and Nagasaki: Early Thinking About Tactical Nuclear Weapons," *International Security* 45, no. 4 (1991): 160.

66. Edmund Russell, "'Speaking of Annihilation': Mobilizing for War Against Human and Insect Enemies," *Journal of American History* 82 (1996): 1520–21; John Dower, *War Without Mercy: Race and Power in the Pacific War* (New York: Pantheon, 1986), 87–88.

67. Fedman and Karacas, "Cartographic Fade to Black," 307, 313–14.

68. TNA, AIR 14/1813, "B–29 Tactical Mission Reports Extracts: Summary," June 10, 1945; Letter for Dr. R. Fisher from London Mission, US Embassy, May 30, 1945.

69. Ralph, "Improvised Destruction," 501.

70. LC, LeMay Papers, Box 16, Air Intelligence report, vol. 1, no. 4, March 29, 1945, 9–10.

71. LC, LeMay Papers, Box 41, notes for a speech to the Ohio Society of New York, November 19, 1945 on "Air Power."

72. McGeorge Bundy, *Danger and Survival: Choices About the Bomb in the First Fifty Years* (New York: Randon House, 1988), 69.

73. Casey, *War Beat, Pacific*, 280.

74. Crane, *American Airpower Strategy*, 183.

75. LC, LeMay Papers, "Phase Analysis, Incendiary Operations," n.d. [but April 1945], 10, 32.

76. Coox, "Strategic Bombing in the Pacific," 322–24.

77. LeMay and Kantor, *Mission with LeMay*, 372.

78. TNA, AIR 48/68, USSBS Report, "Strategic Air Operations," 31; Richard Frank, *Downfall: The End of the Imperial Japanese Empire* (New York: Random House, 1999), 78–79. Frank has a slightly different figure for mines dropped by the command: 13,102.

79. LC, LeMay Papers, Box 16, XXI Bomber Command Activity Report, July 1, 1945, 2.

80. Schwabe, *Burning Japan*, 134.

81. Yorifusa, "Japanese Cities and Planning," 17; Werrell, *Blankets of Fire*, 141.

82. LC, LeMay Papers, Box 16, XXI Bomber Command Activity Report, July 1, 1945, 2.

83. Henry Arnold, *Global Mission* (New York: Harper & Row, 1949), 596. Bomber statistics from TNA AIR 48/68, "Strategic Air Operations," Appendix, 5.

84. Schwabe, *Burning Japan*, 137–39.

85. Nicholas Sarantakes, "The Royal Air Force on Okinawa: The Diplomacy of a Coalition on the Verge of Victory," *Diplomatic History* 27, no. 4 (2003): 484–86, 495.

86. TNA, WO 193/694, Joint Staff Mission, Washington DC to AMSSO, June 5, 1944; JSM to AMSSO, October 27, 1944; Chiefs of Staff meeting, March 19, 1945; War Cabinet, Joint Planning Staff, "Revised Plans for V. L.R. Bomber Force," April 28, 1945.

87. TNA, AIR 9/433, AVM Lloyd to Undersecretary of State, Air Ministry, May 6, 1945; Assistant Chief of Air Staff to Director of Plans, Air Ministry, May 5, 1945.

88. TNA, HO 196/30, RE8 Report, "Area Attacks Against Japan," May 25, 1945, 2–3.

89. Sarantakes, "Royal Air Force on Okinawa," 483.

90. TNA, WO 193/694, Churchill to King, June 16, 1945.

91. TNA, AIR 9/433, Portal to Eaker, May 13, 1945.

92. TNA, AIR 20/5054, "Report of the Fourth Visit to Washington and the Pacific by AVM Lloyd," July 23, 1945, 5; AIR 9/434, Lloyd to Air Ministry, June 24, 1945; AVM Satterley to Lloyd, June 24, 1945 (from Manila).

93. TNA, AIR 20/5054, Churchill to Marshall, June 12, 1945; Thomas Hall, "'Mere Drops in the Ocean': The Politics and Planning of the Contribution of the British Commonwealth to the Final Defeat of Japan, 1944–5," *Diplomacy and Statecraft* 16 (2005): 109.

94. TNA, AIR 9/434, Chiefs of Staff meeting July 9, 1945; AIR 20/5054, "Estimated Deployment of the 'Tiger Force' Heavy Bomber Squadrons in the Pacific," June 15, 1945.

95. TNA, HO 338/7, Report by British Mission to Japan, "The Bombing of Japan," October 18, 1946.

96. LC, LeMay Papers, Box 37, HQ XX Air Force, "Operations Cumulative Through 14 August 1945."

97. Werrell, *Blankets of Fire*, 237–38, 257, 264.

98. Huston, *American Air Power Comes of Age*, 326, Arnold diary entry for June 13, 1945; Ralph, "Improvised Destruction," 515.

99. Frank, *Downfall*, 304–7.

100. USSBS, Pacific Theater, "The Effects of Strategic Bombing on Japan's War Economy," December 1946, 180–81.

101. TNA, AIR 48/68, USSBS Final Report, September 1, 1946, 30–31.

102. Masayasu Miyazaki and Osamu Itō, "The Transformation of Industries in the War Years," in *Economic History of Japan 1914–1955*, ed. Takafusa Nakamura and Konosuke Odaka (Oxford: Oxford University Press, 1999), 321–23.

103. TNA, HO 338/7, British Mission to Japan Report "The Bombing of Japan," October 18, 1946, 4.

104. USSBS, "Summary Report (Pacific War)," July 1, 1946, 21.

105. Department of the Army Air Forces, "Mission Accomplished: Interrogations of Japanese Industrial, Military, and Civil Leaders of World War II," Washington, DC, 1946, 72.

106. Ferenc Szasz, "'Pamphlets Away': The Allied Propaganda Campaign over Japan During the Last Months of World War II," *Journal of Popular Culture* 42, no. 3 (2009): 532–36; Leo Margolin, *Paper Bullets: A Brief Story of Psychological Warfare in World War II* (New York: Froben Press, 1946), 127–28; Patrick Porter, "Paper Bullets: American Psywar in the Pacific, 1944–1945," *War in History* 17, no. 4 (2010): 498–99, 508–9. On psychological warfare and bombing in Europe, see Richard Overy, "Making and Breaking Morale: British Political Warfare and Bomber Command During the Second World War," *Twentieth Century British History* 26, no. 3 (2015): 389–92.

107. Truman Library, Atomic Bomb Collection, Box 1, OPD "Military Use of the Atomic Bomb," 16–17; Edward Miller, *War Plan Orange:*

The U. S. Strategy to Defeat Japan 1897–1945 (Annapolis, MD: Naval Institute Press, 1991), 365.

108. Truman Library, Atomic Bomb Collection, Box 1, Minutes of meeting at the White House on War Strategy, June 18, 1945, 6; Coox, "Strategic Bombing in the Pacific," 340.

109. Details of the planning in Frank, *Downfall*, 117–19.

CHAPTER 3: WHY THE ATOMIC BOMBS?

1. Charles Thorpe, "Against Time: Scheduling, Momentum, and Moral Order at Wartime Los Alamos," *Journal of Historical Sociology* 17, no. 1 (2004): 47, citing Wilson's article "Conscience of a Physicist," in *Alamogordo Plus Twenty-Five Years*, ed. Richard Lewis and Jane Wilson (New York: Viking, 1971).

2. McGeorge Bundy, *Danger and Survival: Choices About the Bomb in the First Fifty Years* (New York: Random House, 1988), 60.

3. Thorpe, "Against Time," 48.

4. Graham Farmelo, *Churchill's Bomb: A Hidden History of Britain's First Nuclear Weapons Programme* (London: Faber & Faber, 2013), 179–91.

5. Stephen Chiabotti, "Complementarity, Correspondence, and the Community of the Bomb," *Journal of American-East Asian Relations* 4, no. 2 (1995): 139.

6. Ray Monk, *Inside the Centre: The Life of J. Robert Oppenheimer* (London: Jonathan Cape, 2012), 450; Sean Malloy, "'The Rules of Civilized Warfare': Scientists, Soldiers, Civilians, and American Nuclear Targeting, 1940–1945," *Journal of Strategic Studies* 30, no. 3 (2007): 482–83.

7. William Miscamble, *The Most Controversial Decision: Truman, the Atom Bomb, and the Defeat of Japan* (Cambridge: Cambridge University Press, 2011), 7; Farmelo, *Churchill's Bomb*, 141–43.

8. Andrew Rotter, *Hiroshima: The World's Bomb* (Oxford: Oxford University Press, 2008), 88–94.

9. Warren Kimball, ed., *Churchill & Roosevelt: The Complete Correspondence: Volume I, Alliance Emerging* (London: Collins, 1984),

249–50, 279, letter Bush to Churchill, October 11, 1941; Churchill to Roosevelt, December 1941. Churchill replied only in early December without any commitment beyond a "readiness to collaborate."

10. R. V. Jones, "Churchill and Science," in *Churchill*, ed. Robert Blake and Wm. Roger Louis (Oxford: Oxford University Press, 1993), 438.

11. Monk, *Inside the Centre*, 322.

12. Leslie Groves, *Now It Can Be Told: The Story of the Manhattan Project* (New York: Harper & Row, 1962), 3–5, 10–12, 17; Miscamble, *Most Controversial Decision*, 8.

13. Monk, *Inside the Centre*, 303.

14. Richard Rhodes, *The Making of the Atomic Bomb* (New York: Simon & Schuster, 1986), 448.

15. William Laurence, *Dawn over Zero: The Story of the Atomic Bomb* (New York: Knopf, 1946), 181–82; Lindsey Banco, "The Biographies of J. Robert Oppenheimer: Desert Saint or Destroyer of Worlds," *Biography* 35, no. 3 (2012): 505.

16. Groves, *Now It Can Be Told*, 66–67, 150.

17. Kai Bird and Martin Sherwin, *American Prometheus: The Triumph and Tragedy of J. Robert Oppenheimer* (New York: Knopf, 2005), 540–41.

18. Mark Fiege, "The Atomic Scientists, the Sense of Wonder, and the Bomb," *Environmental History* 12, no. 3 (2007): 579.

19. Fiege, "Atomic Scientists," 584–86, 599–600.

20. Hans Bethe and Robert Christy, "Oppie's Colleagues Affirm His Leadership in Manhattan Project," *Physics Today* 53, no. 6 (2000): 15.

21. Monk, *Inside the Centre*, 350–52.

22. Bethe and Christy, "Oppie's Colleagues," 15.

23. Ferenc Szasz, *British Scientists and the Manhattan Project: The Los Alamos Years* (London: Macmillan, 1992), xv, xviii, 16–25.

24. Rhodes, *Making of the Atomic Bomb*, 466–67, 573–78; Szasz, *British Scientists*, 23–24.

25. George Kostiakowsky, "Trinity—A Reminiscence," *Bulletin of the Atomic Scientists* 36, no. 6 (1980): 19–20; Monk, *Inside the Centre*, 409–11, 419.

26. Thorpe, "Against Time," 37–42; Bethe and Christy, "Oppie's Colleagues," 15.

27. Malloy, "'Rules of Civilized Warfare,'" 484–89.

28. Bundy, *Danger and Survival*, 90; J. Samuel Walker, *Prompt and Utter Destruction: Truman and the Use of the Atomic Bomb Against Japan* (Chapel Hill: University of North Carolina Press, 2016), 13.

29. Walker, *Prompt and Utter Destruction*, 13–14.

30. Truman Library, "Decision to Drop the Atomic Bomb Collection," Target Committee Report to Groves, May 12, 1945, 1–6; Rhodes, *Making of the Atomic Bomb*, 627–28.

31. Malloy, "'Rules of Civilized Warfare,'" 492.

32. The National Archives, Kew, London (hereafter TNA), CAB 126/250, Field Marshal Wilson to Anderson, May 30, 1945, enclosing "Outline Plan," 1–2.

33. Truman Library, "Decision to Drop the Bomb Collection," Notes of the Interim Committee Meeting, June 1, 1945, 8–9; Henry Stimson, "The Decision to Use the Atomic Bomb," *Harper's Magazine*, February 1947; Sean Malloy, *Atomic Tragedy: Henry L. Stimson and the Decision to Use the Atomic Bomb Against Japan* (Ithaca, NY: Cornell University Press, 2008), 114–17.

34. Monk, *Inside the Centre*, 429–31, 434–35.

35. Szasz, *British Scientists*, 31 (attributed to Peggy Titterton, wife of a British scientist attached to the project).

36. Szasz, *British Scientists*, 403.

37. Chiabotti, "Complementarity, Correspondence," 134; Thorpe, "Against Time," 43–44; Monk, *Inside the Centre*, 432–34.

38. Rotter, *Hiroshima*, 147–51.

39. Jason Kelly, "Why Did Henry Stimson Spare Kyoto from the Bomb?," *Journal of American-East Asian Relations* 19, no. 2 (2012): 188–90, 201–2.

40. Kenneth Bainbridge, "1975: All in Our Time: A Foul and Awesome Display," *Bulletin of the Atomic Scientists* 71, no. 6 (2020): 374–75.

41. Kostiakowsky, "Trinity—A Reminiscence," 19–21; Bainbridge, "1975: All in Our Time," 375–77.

42. Phillips O'Brien, "The Joint Chiefs of Staff, the Atom Bomb, the American Military Mind, and the End of the Second World War," *Journal of Strategic Studies* 42, no. 7 (2019): 981–83, 985–87.

43. TNA, CAB 101/45, John Ehrman manuscript, "The Atomic Bomb: An Account of British Policy in the Second World War," July 1953, 251.

44. Rotter, *Hiroshima*, 159.

45. Bainbridge, "1975: All in Our Time," 377–79; Fiege, "Atomic Scientists," 601.

46. Monk, *Inside the Centre*, 440; Bird and Sherwin, *American Prometheus*, 308–9.

47. Bainbridge, "1975: All in Our Time," 379; Laurence, *Dawn over Zero*, 7.

48. Jennett Conant, *109, East Palace: Robert Oppenheimer and the Secret City of Los Alamos* (New York: Simon & Schuster, 2005), 316–17.

49. TNA, CAB 126/250, Washington Embassy to War Cabinet Offices, July 18, 1945, "Initial Report by Sir James Chadwick, 16 July 1945"; Chadwick to Anderson, July 23, 1945, 2.

50. Truman Library, Atomic Bomb Collection, Groves to Stimson, July 18, 1945, 1, 8.

51. Monk, *Inside the Centre*, 441; Alex Wellerstein, "The Kyoto Misconception: What Truman Knew, and Didn't Know, About Hiroshima," in *The Age of Hiroshima*, ed. Michael Gordin and G. John Ikenberry (Princeton, NJ: Princeton University Press, 2020), 42; Farmelo, *Churchill's Bomb*, 300; Walker, *Prompt and Utter Destruction*, 58.

52. TNA, CAB 127/37, Hastings Ismay to Churchill, November 8, 1944; Ismay to Anderson, January 6, 1945; Anderson to Churchill, January 10, 1945. Lindemann quotation in Farmelo, *Churchill's Bomb*, 286.

53. TNA, CAB 127/37, Anderson to Churchill, May 2, 1945; CAB 101/45, Ehrman manuscript "The Atomic Bomb," 253–58; Jonathan Rosenberg, "Before the Bomb and After: Winston Churchill and the Use of Force," in *Cold War Statesmen Confront the Bomb: Diplomacy Since 1945*, ed. John Gaddis (Oxford: Oxford University Press, 1999), 180–81.

54. Wellerstein, "Kyoto Misconception," 41–42.

55. John Huston, ed., *American Airpower Comes of Age: General Henry "Hap" Arnold's World War II Diaries: Volume 2* (Maxwell, AL: Air University Press, 2002), 378, entry for July 22, 1945; 379, entry for July 23, 1945; 380, entry for July 24, 1945.

56. Truman Library, Atomic Bomb Collection, Stone to Arnold, July 24, 1945, "Groves Project," 1.

57. Library of Congress (hereafter LC), Spaatz Papers, I/73, Directive for General Spaatz from the War Dept., July 24, 1945; Spaatz to War Dept., July 25, 1945. The directive was handed to Spaatz, Nimitz, and MacArthur by General Handy.

58. Nicholas Sarantakes, "Warriors of Word and Sword: The Battle of Okinawa, Media Coverage, and Truman's Reevaluation of Strategy in the Pacific," *Journal of American-East Asian Relations* 23–24 (2016): 366.

59. Truman Library, Atomic Bomb Collection, minutes of meeting held in the White House, June 18, 1945, 3–4.

60. D. M. Giangreco, "Casualty Projections for the U.S. Invasion of Japan, 1945–1946: Planning and Policy Implications," *Journal of Military History* 61, no. 3 (1997): 535–45.

61. National Archives and Records Administration, RG107, Box 139, "United States Chemical Warfare Committee: Periodic Report of Readiness for Chemical Warfare as of 1 January 1945," 3, 12, 49–50, 123–24.

62. John van Courtland Moon, "Project SPHINX: The Question of the Use of Gas in the Planned Invasion of Japan," *Journal of Strategic Studies* 12, no. 3 (1989): 304–9.

63. Laurence, *Dawn over Zero*, 187.

64. Barton Bernstein, "Eclipsed by Hiroshima and Nagasaki: Early Thinking About Tactical Nuclear Weapons," *International Security* 15, no. 4 (1991): 149–51, 160–61.

65. Douglas MacEachin, *The Final Months of the War with Japan: Signals Intelligence, U.S. Invasion Planning, and the A-Bomb Decision* (Washington, DC: Center for the Study of Intelligence, 1998), 6–8,

17–22; Richard Frank, *Downfall: The End of the Imperial Japanese Empire* (New York: Random House, 1999), 148, 212–13.

66. Hasegawa Tsuyoshi, "Were the Atomic Bombings Justified?," in *Bombing Civilians: A Twentieth-Century History*, ed. Yuki Tanaka and Marilyn Young (New York: New Press, 2009), 119.

67. David Earhart, *Certain Victory: Images of World War II in the Japanese Media* (New York: Routledge, 2003), 441–43.

68. Alvin Coox, "The Enola Gay and Japan's Struggle to Surrender," *Journal of American-East Asian Relations* 4, no. 2 (1995): 163; Ben-Ami Shillony, *Politics and Culture in Wartime Japan* (Oxford: Oxford University Press, 1981), 82–84.

69. TNA, CAB 101/45, Ehrman manuscript, "The Atomic Bomb," 230.

70. For an excellent summary of these arguments, see Marc Gallicchio, *Unconditional: The Japanese Surrender in World War II* (Oxford: Oxford University Press, 2020), 51–57.

71. Gallicchio, *Unconditional*, 118–21; TNA, CAB 101/45, Ehrman manuscript, "The Atomic Bomb," 260–62.

72. Malloy, *Atomic Tragedy*, 125.

73. Richard Frank, *Downfall: The End of the Imperial Japanese Empire* (New York: Random House, 1999), 224–25. Frank places great emphasis on these intercepts as evidence that there was no desire for unconditional surrender, though they do indicate a desire to terminate the war.

74. Gallicchio, *Unconditional*, 66, 77–79, 120.

75. Walker, *Prompt and Utter Destruction*, 69; Gallicchio, *Unconditional*, 123.

76. Gar Alperovitz, *Atomic Diplomacy: Hiroshima and Potsdam* (New York: Simon & Schuster, 1965). Alperovitz summed up the decades of subsequent argument over his thesis in *The Decision to Use the Atomic Bomb* (New York: Knopf, 1995), 643–68, "Afterword."

77. David Holloway, "Jockeying for Position in the Postwar World," in *The End of the Pacific War: Reappraisals*, ed. Hasegawa Tsuyoshi (Stanford, CA: Stanford University Press, 2007), 167–68; Campbell Craig and Sergey Radchenko, *The Atomic Bomb and the Origin of the Cold War* (New Haven, CT: Yale University Press, 2008), 58.

78. Geoffrey Roberts, *Stalin's Wars from World War I to Cold War, 1939–1945* (New Haven, CT: Yale University Press, 2006), 282–84.

79. James Matray, "Potsdam Revisited: Prelude to a Divided Korea," *Journal of American-East Asian Relations* 24 (2017): 262–64; Holloway, "Jockeying for Position," 165.

80. Rudolf Janssens, *"What Future for Japan?": U.S. Wartime Planning for the Postwar Era, 1942–1945* (Amsterdam: University of Amsterdam, 1995), 320.

81. Walker, *Prompt and Utter Destruction*, 56.

82. Sean McMeekin, *Stalin's War* (London: Allen Lane, 2021), 640–41; Holloway, "Jockeying for Position," 172.

83. Matray, "Potsdam Revisited," 271–72, 276; Roberts, *Stalin's Wars*, 293.

84. Farmelo, *Churchill's Bomb*, 303; Craig and Radchenko, *The Atomic Bomb*, xx–xxii.

85. TNA, FO 800/555, Moscow embassy (A. Clark Kerr) to Foreign Office, September 10, 1945; Moscow embassy to Foreign Office, October 26, 1945; Holloway, "Jockeying for Position," 185.

86. Moon, "Project SPHINX," 303.

87. Steven Casey, *The War Beat, Pacific: The American Media at War Against Japan* (Oxford: Oxford University Press, 2021), 282; Walker, *Prompt and Utter Destruction*, 98.

88. Truman Library, Atomic Bomb Collection, Notes of the Interim Committee Meeting, June 1, 1945, 9.

89. Bernstein, "Eclipsed by Hiroshima and Nagasaki," 156.

90. Sean Malloy, "'A Very Pleasant Way to Die': Radiation Effects and the Decision to Use the Bomb Against Japan," *Diplomatic History* 36, no. 3 (2012): 516–17.

91. LC, Arnold Papers, Reel 199, "Atomic Bomb Cities," July 25, 1945.

92. Truman Library, Atomic Bomb Collection, Stone to Arnold, July 24, 1945, on "Groves Project."

93. Bundy, *Danger and Survival*, 77–79.

94. Wellerstein, "Kyoto Misconception," 42, 45.

95. Szasz, *British Scientists and the Manhattan Project*, 27.

96. The above paragraph from Groves, *Now It Can Be Told*, 258–60, 278–83.

97. Laurence, *Dawn over Zero*, 198, 203–4.

98. TNA, CAB 126/250, Field Marshal Wilson to Anderson, August 21, 1945; Cheshire memorandum "The Atomic Bomb Project: American Reaction to the Presence of British Representatives at Tinian," August 18, 1945.

99. Laurence, *Dawn over Zero*, 204.

100. Frank Barnaby, "The Effects of the Atomic Bombings of Hiroshima and Nagasaki," *Medicine and War* 11, no. 3 (1995): 2–4.

101. Civil Defense Liaison Office, "Fire Effects of Bombing Attacks," National Security Resources Board, August 1951, 24–26.

102. Civil Defense Liaison Office, "Fire Effects of Bombing Attacks," 21. The temperature for a brief moment was calculated to be 70 million °C.

103. Andrew Weale, ed., *Hiroshima: First-Hand Accounts of the Atomic Terror That Changed the World* (London: Robinson Publishing, 1995), 156–57.

104. Setsuko Thurlow, "Hiroshima: A Survivor's Testimony," *Irish Studies in International Affairs* 25 (2014): 14.

105. The Committee for the Compilation of Materials on Damage Caused by the Atomic Bombs on Hiroshima and Nagasaki, *Hiroshima and Nagasaki: The Physical, Medical, and Social Effects of the Atomic Bombings* (London: Hutchinson, 1981), 113; Yuko Matsunari and Nao Yoshimoto, "Comparison of Rescue and Relief Activities Within 72 Hours of the Atomic Bombings in Hiroshima and Nagasaki," *Prehospital and Disaster Medicine* 28, no. 6 (2013): 537–38.

106. Harry S. Truman, *Year of Decision, 1945: The Memoirs of Harry S. Truman, Volume I* (London: Hodder & Stoughton, 1955), 351–52; Truman Library, Atomic Bomb Collection, Admiral Edwards to William Leahy, August 6, 1945; Stimson to Truman, August 6, 1945.

107. H. G. Nicholas, ed., *Washington Despatches, 1944–45: Weekly Political Reports from the British Embassy* (London: Weidenfeld & Nicolson, 1981), 398.

108. Truman Library, Atomic Bomb Collection, President's Secretary's files, "Draft Statement on the Dropping of the Bomb, July 30, 1945," 3.

109. Monk, *Inside the Centre*, 451; Jonathan Rosenberg, "Before the Bomb and After: Winston Churchill and the Use of Force," in *Cold War Statesmen Confront the Bomb: Diplomacy Since 1945*, ed. John Gaddis (Oxford: Oxford University Press, 1999), 182.

110. Henry DeWolf Smyth, *Atomic Energy for Military Purposes* (Princeton, NJ: Princeton University Press, 1948). The quotation comes from the Princeton publicity, but it reflects the tenor of the book, which says nothing about the two bombs that were dropped on Japan. The draft was circulated by the army in August 1945 and later published by Princeton.

111. Wellerstein, "Kyoto Misconception," 53.

112. Robert Rhodes James, "The Parliamentarian, Orator, Statesman," in *Churchill*, ed. Robert Blake and Wm. Roger Louis (Oxford: Oxford University Press, 1993), 516.

CHAPTER 4: SURRENDER

1. Noriko Kawamura, *Emperor Hirohito and the Pacific War* (Seattle: University of Washington Press, 2015), 183, letter to his twelve-year-old son.

2. David Earhart, *Certain Victory: Images of World War II in the Japanese Media* (New York: Routledge, 2008), 1, 11.

3. Pacific War Research Society, *Japan's Longest Day* (Palo Alto, CA: Kodansha International, 1968).

4. Kawamura, *Emperor Hirohito*, 142; Earhart, *Certain Victory*, 429, 461.

5. Truman Library, Atomic Bomb Collection, Box 1, "Military Use of Atomic Bombs," Report Based on OPD Records, n.d., 15–16.

6. Owen Griffiths, "Need, Greed, and Protest in Japan's Black Market," *Journal of Social History* 35 (2002): 832.

7. Earhart, *Certain Victory*, 409–10, 443–44.

8. Erich Pauer, "The Broken Axis—8 May 1945 in Japan," in *Japan and Germany*, vol. 1, ed. Akira Kudō, Tajima Nobuo, and Erich Pauer (Leiden: Brill, 2009), 534–36.

9. Details all from Andrew Levidis, "The War is Not Over: Kishi Nobusuke and the National Defense Brotherhood, 1944–5," *Journal of Japanese Studies* 49, no. 1 (2023): 4–24.

10. Truman Library, Atomic Bomb Collection, Box 1, Stimson to Truman, July 2, 1945, encl. "Proposed Program for Japan," 4.

11. Richard Frank, *Downfall: The End of the Imperial Japanese Empire* (New York: Random House, 1999), 89.

12. Kawamura, *Emperor Hirohito*, 143–45.

13. Jeremy Yellen, "The Specter of Revolution: Reconsidering Japan's Decision to Surrender," *International History Review* 35, no. 1 (2013): 211.

14. Yukiko Koshiro, "Eurasian Eclipse: Japan's End Game in World War II," *American Historical Review* 109, no. 2 (2004): 428–34.

15. Earhart, *Certain Victory*, 323.

16. Janice Matsumura, "Internal Security in Wartime Japan (1937–45) and the Creation of Internal Insecurity," *Canadian Journal of History* 31, no. 3 (1996): 408–10.

17. David Ambaras, "Juvenile Delinquency and the National Defense State: Policing Young Workers in Wartime Japan, 1937–1945," *Journal of Asian Studies* 63, no. 1 (2004): 31–37.

18. Saburō Ienya, *The Pacific War 1931–1945* (New York: Random House, 1978), 216–21, 229–30; Ben-Ami Shillony, *Politics and Culture in Wartime Japan* (Oxford: Oxford University Press, 1981), 106.

19. This and the above paragraph from Kawamura, *Emperor Hirohito*, 145–49, 154–56.

20. Gary Bass, *Judgment at Tokyo: World War II on Trial and the Making of Modern Asia* (New York: Knopf, 2023), 48.

21. Rudolf Janssens, *"What Future for Japan?": U. S. Wartime Planning for the Postwar Era 1942–1945* (Amsterdam: University of Amsterdam, 1995), 120–22, 130–33, 229–34; Eric Fowler, "Will-to-Fight: Japan's Imperial Institution and the United States Strategy to End World War II," *War and Society* 34 (2015): 47–48.

22. Uday Mohan and Sanho Tree, "Hiroshima, the American Media, and the Construction of Conventional Wisdom," *Journal of American-East*

Asian Relations 4, no. 2 (1995): 141–47, 149–51; Kase Toshikazu, *Eclipse of the Rising Sun* (London: Jonathan Cape, 1951), 197.

23. Kawamura, *Emperor Hirohito*, 159–60; Marc Gallicchio, *Unconditional: The Japanese Surrender in World War II* (Oxford: Oxford University Press, 2020), 92–93.

24. Louis Allen, "Japan Surrenders: Reason and Unreason in August 1945," in *War, Conflict, and Security in Japan and Asia-Pacific, 1941–52*, ed. Ian Nish and Mark Allen (Folkestone, Kent: Global Oriental, 2011), 145. The translations from the "Monologue" were made by Louis Allen.

25. Kase, *Eclipse of the Rising Sun*, 172–73; Shillony, *Politics and Culture in Wartime Japan*, 84.

26. Takafusa Nakamura, "The Age of Turbulence: 1937–54," in *Economic History of Japan 1914–1955*, ed. Takafusa Nakamura and Kōnosuke Odaka (Oxford: Oxford University Press, 1999), 80.

27. Nakamura, "Age of Turbulence," 70, 80–81.

28. Masayasu Miyazaki and Osamu Itō, "Transformation of Industries in War Years," in *Economic History of Japan 1914–1955*, ed. Takafusa Nakamura and Kōnosuke Odaka (Oxford: Oxford University Press, 1999), 328–29.

29. Bruce Johnston, *Japanese Food Management in World War II* (Stanford, CA: Stanford University Press, 1953), 156–57, 251; Chris Aldous, "Contesting Famine: Hunger and Nutrition in Occupied Japan, 1945–1952," *Journal of American-East Asian Relations* 17, no. 3 (2010): 236–38; Owen Griffiths, "Need, Greed, and Protest in Japan's Black Market," *Journal of Social History* 35 (2002): 827–32.

30. Hibiki Yamaguchi, "US Prisoners of War in Hiroshima," *Journal of Peace and Nuclear Disarmament* 2, no. 1 (2019): 82.

31. Yellen, "Specter of Revolution," 213–17; Samuel Yamashita, *Daily Life in Wartime Japan* (Lawrence: University of Kansas Press, 2015), 37–39, 44–45.

32. Thomas Havens, *Valley of Darkness: The Japanese People and World War Two* (New York: Norton, 1978), 190.

33. Sheldon Garon, "On the Transnational Destruction of Cities," *Past and Present* 247 (2020): 265–68.

34. Havens, *Valley of Darkness*, 190.

35. Allen, "Japan Surrenders," 145. The reference comes from the "Monologue." The report was supplied by Adm. Hasegawa Kiyoshi.

36. Kase, *Eclipse of the Rising Sun*, 180–85; Yellen, "Specter of Revolution," 213–14; Kawamura, *Emperor Hirohito*, 156–59.

37. Justin Libby, "The Search for a Negotiated Peace: Japanese Diplomats' Attempt to Surrender Japan Prior to the Bombing of Hiroshima and Nagasaki," *World Affairs* 156, no. 1 (1993): 36–39; Janssens, *"What Future for Japan?,"* 276–78; Gerhard Krebs, "Operation Super-Sunrise? Japanese-United States Peace Feelers in Switzerland, 1945," *Journal of Military History* 69 (2005): 1087–96.

38. Koshiro, "Eurasian Eclipse," 434.

39. Kase, *Eclipse of the Rising Sun*, 180; Hasegawa Tsuyoshi, "Soviet Policy Toward Japan in World War II," *Cahiers du monde russe*, 52, nos. 2–3 (2011): 5–6.

40. The National Archives, Kew, London (hereafter TNA), CAB 101/45, Ehrman manuscript, "The Atomic Bomb," 259.

41. On the interpretation of *mokusatsu*, see the appendix in Allen, "Japan Surrenders," 161–62.

42. Kase, *Eclipse of the Rising Sun*, 210.

43. Mohan and Tree, "Hiroshima," 156.

44. Truman Library, Atomic Bomb Collection, OPD Report "Military Use of the Atomic Bomb," 3–4, 42–43.

45. TNA, CAB 126/252, Manhattan Engineer District, "The Atomic Bombings of Hiroshima and Nagasaki," June 29, 1946, 2.

46. Truman Library, Atomic Bomb Collection, "Leaflet Dropped on Japanese Cities (AB–11) in Connection with the Atomic Bombs."

47. Kenneth Werrell, *Blankets of Fire: U. S. Bombers over Japan During World War II* (Washington, DC: Smithsonian, 1996), 207–8; Warren Kozak, *LeMay: The Life and Wars of General Curtis LeMay* (Washington, DC: Regnery, 2009), 255; Ward Wilson, "The

Winning Weapon? Rethinking Nuclear Weapons in Light of Hiroshima," *International Security* 31, no. 4 (2007): 169.

48. Tristan Grunow, "A Reexamination of the 'Shock of Hiroshima': The Japanese Bomb Projects and Surrender Reconsidered," *Journal of American-East Asia Relations* 12, nos. 3–4 (2003): 164–66.

49. Shillony, *Politics and Culture in Wartime Japan*, 106–7.

50. Shillony, *Politics and Culture in Wartime Japan*, 173–74.

51. Alvin Coox, "The Enola Gay and Japan's Struggle to Surrender," *Journal of American-East Asian Relations* 4, no. 2 (1995): 166.

52. TNA, CAB 126/250, "Report of Investigation on Hiroshima Air Raid Damage, August 13, 1945," 1–3; "Report on the Hiroshima Catastrophe," August 15, 1945, 7 (both translated from the Japanese).

53. Hatano Sumio, "The Atomic Bomb and Soviet Entry into the War: Of Equal Importance," in *The End of the Pacific War: Reappraisals*, ed. Hasegawa Tsuyoshi (Stanford, CA: Stanford University Press, 2007), 98–99.

54. Grunow, "A Reconsideration," 175–76.

55. Wilson, "The Winning Weapon?," 166.

56. Alexander Hill, ed., *The Great Patriotic War of the Soviet Union* (London: Routledge, 2008), 205–11.

57. Francis Pike, *Hirohito's War: The Pacific War 1941–1945* (London: Bloomsbury, 2015), 1080–81; G. F. Krivosheev, ed., *Soviet Casualties and Combat Losses in the Twentieth Century* (London: Greenhill Books, 1997), 160–61.

58. Hatano, "The Atomic Bomb," 99–100.

59. Allen, "Japan Surrenders," 148.

60. On this issue there is some disagreement among historians over whether Hirohito did or did not refer to the bomb in this speech, but the other factors, including the persistent air raids and the effect on the home population, were important enough in explaining the decision. The record of this and other meetings were set down afterward, sometimes contemporaneously, sometimes well after the event. The reliability of much of this evidence has to be treated cautiously.

61. Kawamura, *Emperor Hirohito*, 163–66; Hatano, "The Atomic Bomb," 104–6; Yellen, "Specter of Revolution," 216–17.

62. Rinjirō Sodei, "Hiroshima/Nagasaki in History and Politics," *Journal of American History* 82 (1995): 1119.

63. Library of Congress, Spaatz Papers, I/73, Directive for General Spaatz from the War Dept., July 24, 1945.

64. TNA, CAB 126/250, US Information Service, "Eye-Witness Account of Atomic Bombing of Nagasaki," September 11, 1945, 3.

65. Steven Casey, *The War Beat, Pacific: The American Media at War Against Japan* (Oxford: Oxford University Press, 2021), 288.

66. Committee for Compilation of Materials on Damage Caused by the Atomic Bombs on Hiroshima and Nagasaki, *Hiroshima and Nagasaki: The Physical, Medical, and Social Effects of the Atomic Bombings* (London: Hutchinson, 1981), 27–29, 57, 63–66, 114.

67. Yuko Matsunari and Nao Yoshimoto, "Comparison of Rescue and Relief Activities Within 72 Hours of the Atomic Bombings in Hiroshima and Nagasaki," *Prehospital and Disaster Medicine* 28, no. 6 (2013): 538–41.

68. Takashi Nagai, *We of Nagasaki* (London: Gollancz, 1951), 53–54.

69. Committee for Compilation of Materials, *Hiroshima and Nagasaki*, 503–4.

70. Ray Monk, *Inside the Centre: The Life of J. Robert Oppenheimer* (London: Jonathan Cape, 2012), 455.

71. Truman Library, Decision to Use the Atomic Bomb Collection, Truman to Cavert, August 11, 1945; Truman to Richard Russell, August 9, 1945.

72. H. G. Nicholas, ed., *Washington Despatches 1944–5: Weekly Political Reports from the British Embassy* (London: Weidenfeld & Nicolson, 1981), 602.

73. Nicholas, *Washington Despatches*, 599.

74. Monk, *Inside the Centre*, 457–58.

75. Barton Bernstein, "Eclipsed by Hiroshima and Nagasaki: Early Thinking About Tactical Nuclear Weapons," *International Security* 15, no. 4 (1991): 165–67; Barton Bernstein, "Reconsidering the 'Atomic General': Leslie R. Groves," *Journal of Military History* 67, no. 3 (2003): 907.

76. Janssens, *"What Future for Japan?,"* 318–20.

77. McGeorge Bundy, *Danger and Survival: Choices About the Bomb in the First Fifty Years* (New York: Random House, 1988), 84; Nicholas, *Washington Despatches*, 603.

78. Kawamura, *Emperor Hirohito*, 168–70.

79. Frank, *Downfall*, 297.

80. Levidis, "The War Is Not Over," 1–2, 26–28; Kawamura, *Emperor Hirohito*, 178–79.

81. Pacific War Research Society, *Japan's Longest Day*, 66–71; Kawamura, *Emperor Hirohito*, pp. 174–5.

82. Allen, "Japan Surrenders," 149.

83. Kawamura, *Emperor Hirohito*, 176–77.

84. Earhart, *Certain Victory*, 444–46.

85. Takashi Nagai, *We of Nagasaki*, p. 134.

86. James Matray, "Potsdam Revisited: Prelude to a Divided Korea," *Journal of American-East Asian Relations* 24 (2017): 275–76.

87. Hasegawa, "Soviet Policy Toward Japan," 13–16.

88. Nicholas, *Washington Despatches*, 603, report of August 25, 1945.

89. Earhart, *Certain Victory*, 465–66.

90. Kase, *Eclipse of the Rising Sun*, 261–64; Gallicchio, *Unconditional*, 165–67.

91. Kase, *Eclipse of the Rising Sun*, 265.

92. Hal Brands, "The Emperor's New Clothes: American Views of Hirohito After World War II," *The Historian*, 68, no. 1 (2006), 1–4, 11–12.

93. Brian Walsh, "Japanese Foreign Ministry's Document Destruction Order of 7 August 1945," *Journal of American-East Asian Relations* 26 (2019): 88.

94. Peter Mauch, "Emperor Hirohito's Postwar Reflections," *Journal of American-East Asian Relations* 29, no. 2 (2022): 221–24.

CHAPTER 5: AFTERMATH

1. Kazuyo Yamane, "Current Attitudes to the Atomic Bombing of Japan," *Medicine, Conflict, and Survival* 11, no. 3 (1995): 48.

2. Asado Sadao, "The Mushroom Cloud and National Psyches: Japanese

and American Perceptions of the A-Bomb Decision, 1945–95," *Journal of American-East Asian Relations* 4, no. 2 (1995): 106.

3. Asado Sadao, "The Mushroom Cloud," 104–5.
4. "Text of President Obama's Speech in Hiroshima, Japan," *New York Times*, May 27, 2016.
5. Alex Wellerstein, "The Kyoto Misconception: What Truman Knew, and Didn't Know, About Hiroshima," in *The Age of Hirohito*, ed. Michael Gordin and G. John Ikenberry (Princeton, NJ: Princeton University Press, 2020), 51.
6. Asado Sadao, "The Mushroom Cloud," 102.
7. Katherine McKinney, Scott Sagan, and Allen Weiner, "Why the Atomic Bombing of Hiroshima Would Be Illegal Today," *Bulletin of the Atomic Scientists* 76, no. 4 (2020): 158.
8. Sean Malloy, "'A Very Pleasant Way to Die': Radiation Effects and the Decision to Use the Atomic Bomb Against Japan," *Diplomatic History* 36, no. 3 (2012): 515–17, 541–42.
9. Cary Karacas, "Place, Public Memory, and the Tokyo Air Raids," *Geographical Review* 100, no. 4 (2010): 523; John Dower, "The Bombed: Hiroshima and Nagasaki in Japanese Memory," *Diplomatic History* 19, no. 2 (1995): 281–82.
10. George Roeder, "Making Things Visible: Learning from the Censors," in *Living with the Bomb: American and Japanese Cultural Conflicts in the Nuclear Age*, ed. Laura Hein and Mark Selden (New York: M. E. Sharpe, 1997), 81, 83.
11. U.S. Strategic Bombing Survey (hereafter USSBS), Overall Economic Effects Division, "The Effects of Strategic Bombing on Japan's War Economy," December 1946, 63–65.
12. The National Archives, Kew, London (hereafter TNA), HO 338/7, "The Bombing of Japan," report from the British Mission to Japan on the Effects of Atomic Bombs, October 18, 1946, 4, 7.
13. TNA, AIR 20/5369, Air Ministry to BBSU headquarters, August 18, 1945; Air Ministry to BBSU, August 23, 1945; R. E. Stradling to secretary of the Atomic Energy Advisory Committee, August 28, 1945.
14. TNA, CAB 125/250, "A Report on the Blast Damage Caused by the

Atomic Bomb at Nagasaki" for Prof. Chadwick and General Groves, 15–17; AIR 48/224, Report of the British Mission to Japan on an Investigation of the Effects of the Atomic Bombs Dropped on Hiroshima and Nagasaki," December 1945, 41–47.

15. TNA, CAB 126/252, Manhattan Engineer District, "The Atomic Bombings of Hiroshima and Nagasaki," June 29, 1946, 2–3.

16. Civil Defense Liaison Committee, "Fire Effects of Bombing Attacks," National Security Resources Board, August 1951, 29–36.

17. USSBS, "The Effects of Atomic Bombs on Hiroshima and Nagasaki," in *Fire and the Air War*, ed. Horatio Bond (Boston: National Fire Protection Association, 1946), 234–35.

18. USSBS, "Effects of Atomic Bombs," 221–23.

19. Rinjirō Sodei, "Hiroshima/Nagasaki as History and Politics," *Journal of American History* 82, no. 4 (1995): 1118–19.

20. TNA, FO 800/555, Ambassador A. Clark Kerr to Foreign Office, September 10, 1945; Moscow Embassy to Foreign Office, October 26, 1945; Campbell Craig and Sergey Radchenko, *The Atomic Bomb and the Origins of the Cold War* (New Haven, CT: Yale University Press, 2005), xx–xxiv.

21. TNA, CAB 126/252, Manhattan Engineer District report, 19.

22. TNA, AIR 48/224, Report of the British Mission to Japan, 36–39.

23. Laura Hein and Mark Selden, eds., *Living with the Bomb: American and Japanese Cultural Conflicts in the Nuclear Age* (New York: M. E. Sharpe, 1997), 27.

24. "A Report on Atomic Bomb Survivors' Society in Hiroshima," February 1955, 4; Mark Selden, "American Firebombing and Atomic Bombing of Japan in History and Memory," *Asia-Pacific Journal: Japan Focus* 14, no. 4 (2016): 7–8.

25. Yasuyuki Ohta et al., "Psychological Effect of the Nagasaki Atomic Bombing on Survivors After Half a Century," *Psychiatry and Clinical Neurosciences* 54 (2000): 97–98.

26. Tetsuji Imanaka et al., "Radiation Exposure and Disease Questionnaires of Early Entrants After the Hiroshima Bombing," *Radiation Protection Dosimetry* 149, no. 1 (2012): 91–93.

27. Ran Zwigenberg, *Hiroshima: The Origins of a Global Memory Culture* (Cambridge: Cambridge University Press, 2014), 67–70.

28. Derek Kramer, "An Atomic Age Unleashed: Emancipation and Erasure in Early Korean Accounts of the Hiroshima and Nagasaki Bombings," *Journal of Asian Studies* 82, no. 2 (2023): 145–46, 154–55.

29. Lisa Yoneyama, "Memory Matters: Hiroshima, Korean Atom Bomb Memorial and the Politics of Ethnicity," in *Living with the Bomb: American and Japanese Cultural Conflicts in the Nuclear Age*, ed. Laura Hein and Mark Selden (New York: M. E. Sharpe, 1997), 204–5, 207.

30. John Morris, *The Phoenix Cup: Some Notes on Japan 1946* (London: Cresset Press, 1947), 19, 36–38.

31. Asado Sadao, "The Mushroom Cloud," 95–96.

32. Morris, *The Phoenix Cup*, 61.

33. Owen Griffiths, "Need, Greed, and Protest in Japan's Black Market," *Journal of Social History* 35 (2002): 834–35; Chris Aldous, "Contesting Famine: Hunger and Nutrition in Occupied Japan, 1945–1952," *Journal of American-East Asian Relations* 17, no. 3 (2010): 242–43.

34. Yuki Miyamoto, "Rebirth in the Pure Land or God's Sacrificial Lambs? Religious Interpretations of the Atomic Bombings in Hiroshima and Nagasaki," *Japanese Journal of Religious Studies* 32, no. 1 (2005): 137–39, 143–45.

35. Monica Braw, "Hiroshima and Nagasaki: The Voluntary Silence," in *Living with the Bomb: American and Japanese Cultural Conflicts in the Nuclear Age*, ed. Laura Hein and Mark Selden (New York: M. E. Sharpe, 1997), 165–66.

36. Seiitsu Tachibana, "The Quest for a Peace Culture: The A-Bomb Survivors' Long Struggle for the New Movement for Redressing Foreign Victims of Japan's Wars," *Diplomatic History* 19, no. 2 (1995): 336; "A Report on Atomic Bomb Survivors' Society," 1–2; Masao Tomonaga, "Voices of Nagasaki After 75 Years," *Journal of Peace and Nuclear Disarmament* 4, no. S1 (2021): 277.

37. Akiko Hashimoto, *The Long Defeat: Cultural Trauma, Memory, and Identity in Japan* (Oxford: Oxford University Press, 2015), 2–7; Kazuyo Yamane, "Current Attitudes," 48–49.

38. Masahiko Yamabe, "Thinking Now About the Great Tokyo Air Raid," *Asia-Pacific Journal: Japan Focus* 9, no. 3 (2011): 4–5; Committee for Compilation of Materials on Damage Caused by the Atomic Bombs on Hiroshima and Nagasaki, *Hiroshima and Nagasaki: The Physical, Medical, and Social Effects of the Atomic Bombings* (London: Hutchinson, 1981), 535, 544, 565.

39. Seiitsu Tachibana, "Quest for a Peace Culture," 336–37, 342–44; Kazuyo Yamane, "Current Attitudes," 51; Zwigenberg, *Hiroshima*, 69–70.

40. Asado Sadao, "The Mushroom Cloud," 98; Kazuyo Yamane, "Current Attitudes," 51; Kazuyo Yamane, "Hiroshima and Nagasaki: The Beginning of the Nuclear Age," *Medicine and War* 11, no. 3 (1995): 14.

41. Seiitsu Tachibana, "Quest for a Peace Culture," 337.

42. Masahiko Yamabe, "Thinking Now About the Great Tokyo Air Raid," 1; Karacas, "Place, Public Memory, and the Tokyo Air Raids," 525–26.

43. Karacas, "Place, Memory and the Tokyo Air Raids," 521, 527–32; Bret Fisk and Cary Karacas, "The Firebombing of Tokyo and Its Legacy," *Asia-Pacific Journal: Japan Focus* 9, no. 3 (2011): 3.

44. Laura Hein and Akikio Takenaka, "Exhibiting World War II in Japan and the United States since 1995," *Pacific History Review* 76, no. 1 (2007): 65–70.

45. Henry Stimson, "The Decision to Use the Atomic Bomb," *Harper's Magazine*, February 1947, 9; Martin Sherwin, "Hiroshima as Politics and History," *Journal of American History* 82, no. 4 (1995): 1085–86.

46. David Smith, "U.S. Public Opinion and the Hiroshima and Nagasaki Bombings since 1945," *Peace Review* 32, no. 3 (2020): 342–43.

47. Masaya Nemoto, "Remaking Hiroshima and Nagasaki: Local Commemorations of Atomic Bombings in the United States," *Journal for Peace and Nuclear Disarmament* 2, no. 1 (2019): 39–45.

48. Bryan Hubbard and Marouf Hasian, "The Generic Roots of the Enola Gay Controversy," *Political Communication* 15, no. 1 (1998): 497–503.

49. Sherwin, "Hiroshima as Politics and History," 1070.

50. Yui Daizaburo, "Between Pearl Harbor and Hiroshima/Nagasaki: Nationalism and Memory in Japan and the United States," in *Living with the Bomb: American and Japanese Cultural Conflicts in the Nuclear Age*, ed. Laura Hein and Mark Selden (New York: M. E. Sharpe, 1997), 55–56.

51. Masaya Nemoto, "Remaking Hiroshima and Nagasaki," 37–38.

52. Kazuyo Yamane, "Current Attitudes," 48.

53. Timothy McCormack and Helen Durham, "Aerial Bombardment of Civilians: The Current International Legal Framework," in *Bombing Civilians: A Twentieth-Century History*, ed. Yuki Tanaka and Marilyn Young (New York: New Press, 2009), 226–27.

54. Yuki Miyamoto, *Beyond the Mushroom Cloud: Commemoration, Religion, and Responsibility After Hiroshima* (New York: Fordham University Press, 2012), 8.

55. Harry S. Truman, *Year of Decision, 1945: The Memoirs of Harry S. Truman, Volume I* (London: Hodder & Stoughton, 1955), 350.

56. Craig Cameron, "Race and Identity: The Culture of Combat in the Pacific War," *International History Review* 27, no. 3 (2005): 564.

57. Conrad Crane, "The Evolution of U.S. Strategic Bombing of Urban Areas," *Historian* 50, no. 1 (1987): 36.

58. Joel Hayward, "Air Power, Ethics, and Civilian Immunity During the First World War and Its Aftermath," *Global War Studies* 7 (2010): 127–28; Heinz Hanke, *Luftkrieg und Zivilbevölkerung* (Frankfurt-am-Main: Peter Lang, 1991), 71–77.

59. Theodore Richard, "Nuclear Weapons Targeting: The Evolution of Law and U.S. Policy," *Military Law Review* 224, no. 4 (2016): 881.

60. TNA, AIR 14/249, "Air Ministry Instructions and Notes on the Rules to Be Observed by the Royal Air Force in War," August 17, 1939, 5–7; AIR 41/5, "International Law of the Air 1939–1945," 7.

61. Winston S. Churchill, *The Second World War: Volume II* (London: Cassell, 1957), 567.

62. George Anastapio, *Reflections on Life, Death, and the Constitution* (Lexington: University of Kentucky Press, 2009), 83.

63. McKinney, Sagan, and Weiner, "Why the Atomic Bombing of

Hiroshima Would Be Illegal Today," 158; Richard, "Nuclear Weapons Targeting," 872–73.

64. John Greenwell, "The Atom Bombing of Hiroshima and Nagasaki. Were They War Crimes?," *ISAA Review* 12, no. 2 (2913): 42–43. For an exaggerated view of the principle of reciprocity, see John Bennett, "Reaping the Whirlwind: The Norm of Reciprocity and the Law of Aerial Bombardment in World War II," *Melbourne Journal of International Law* 21 (2020): 305–48.

65. McCormack and Durham, "Aerial Bombardment of Civilians," 220–21.

66. Richard, "Nuclear Weapons Targeting," 900.

67. TNA, DEFE 10/390, Chiefs of Staff JIGSAW Committee, Tenth meeting minutes, February 23, 1960, 1; Twenty-eighth meeting, June 2, 1960; Forty-first meeting, August 4, 1960, 2.

68. McKinney, Sagan, and Weiner, "Why the Atomic Bombing of Hiroshima Would Be Illegal Today," 160–61.

Selected Readings

Akiko Hashimoto. *The Long Defeat: Cultural Trauma, Memory, and Identity in Japan.* Oxford: Oxford University Press, 2015.

Aldous, Chris. "Contesting Famine: Hunger and Nutrition in Occupied Japan, 1945–1952." *Journal of American-East Asian Relations* 17, no. 3 (2010): 230–56.

Alperovitz, Gar. *Atomic Diplomacy: Hiroshima and Potsdam.* New York: Simon & Schuster, 1965.

———. *The Decision to Use the Atomic Bomb.* New York: Random House, 1995.

Arnold, Henry H. *Global Mission.* New York: Harper & Row, 1949.

Asado Sadao. "The Mushroom Cloud and National Psyches: Japanese and American Perceptions of the A-Bomb Decision, 1945–1995." *Journal of American-East Asian Relations* 4, no. 2 (1995): 95–116.

Bass, Gary. *Judgment at Tokyo: World War II on Trial and the Making of Modern Asia.* New York: Knopf, 2023.

Bond, Horatio, ed. *Fire and the Air War.* Boston: National Fire Protection Association, 1946.

Bundy, McGeorge. *Danger and Survival: Choices About the Bomb in the First Fifty Years.* New York: Random House, 1988.

Burgess, Charles. "Pacific Fleet to Singapore? Deterrence, Warfighting, and Anglo-American Plans for the Defense of Southeast Asia, 1937–1941." *Diplomacy and Statecraft* 34, no. 2 (2023): 256–95.

Casey, Stephen. *The War Beat, Pacific: The American Media at War Against Japan.* Oxford: Oxford University Press, 2021.

Chiabotti, Stephen. "Complementarity, Correspondence, and the Community of the Bomb." *Journal of American-East Asian Relations* 4, no. 2 (1995): 129–39.

Coox, Alvin. "Strategic Bombing in the Pacific 1942–1945." In *Case Studies in Strategic Bombardment,* edited by R. Cargill Hall, chap. 4. Washington, DC: Air Force History Program, 1998.

Craig, Campbell, and Sergey Radchenko. *The Atomic Bomb and the Origins of the Cold War.* New Haven, CT: Yale University Press, 2008.

Crane, Conrad. *American Air Power Strategy in World War II: Bombs, Cities, Civilians, and Oil.* Lawrence: University Press of Kansas, 2016.

Dower, John. *Cultures of War: Pearl Harbor, Hiroshima, 9–11, Iraq* (New York: Norton, 2010).

———. *War Without Mercy: Race and Power in the Pacific War.* New York: Pantheon, 1986.

Dunley, Richard. "Rebuilding the Mills of Sea Power: Interwar British Planning for Economic Warfare Against Japan." *International History Review* 44, no. 5 (2022): 1091–107.

Earhart, David. *Certain Victory: Images of World War II in the Japanese Media.* New York: Routledge, 2008.

Earle, Thomas. "'It Made a Lot of Sense to Kill Skilled Workers': The Firebombing of Tokyo in March 1945." *Journal of Military History* 66, no. 1 (2002): 103–33.

Farmelo, Graham. *Churchill's Bomb: A Hidden History of Britain's First Nuclear Weapons Programme.* London: Faber & Faber, 2013.

Fedman, David, and Cary Karacas. "A Cartographic Fade to Black: Mapping the Destruction of Urban Japan During World War II." *Journal of Historical Geography* 38, no. 3 (2012): 306–28.

Fiege, Mark. "The Atomic Scientists, the Sense of Wonder, and the Bomb." *Environmental History* 12, no. 3 (2007): 578–613.

Fisk, Bret. "The Tokyo Air Raids in the Words of Those Who Survived." *Asia-Pacific Journal: Japan Focus* 9, no. 3 (2011): 3471.

Fisk, Bret, and Cary Karacas. "The Firebombing of Tokyo and Its Legacy: Introduction." *Asia-Pacific Journal: Japan Focus* 9, no. 3 (2011): 3469.

Fowler, Eric. "Will-to-Fight: Japan's Imperial Institution and the United States Strategy to End World War II." *War and Society* 34, no. 1 (2015): 43–64.

Frank, Richard. *Downfall: The End of the Imperial Japanese Empire.* New York: Random House, 1999.

Gallicchio, Marc. *Unconditional: The Japanese Surrender in World War II.* Oxford: Oxford University Press, 2020.

Garon, Sheldon. "On the Transnational Destruction of Cities." *Past and Present* 247, no. 1 (2020): 235–71.

Gentile, Gian. "Shaping the Past Battlefield 'For the Future': The United States Strategic Bombing Survey's Evaluation of the American Air War Against Japan." *Journal of Military History* 64, no. 4 (2000): 1085–1112.

Giangreco, D. M. "Casualty Projections for the U. S. Invasions of Japan, 1945–1946: Planning and Policy Implications." *Journal of Military History* 61, no. 3 (1997): 521–82.

Gladwell, Malcolm. *The Bomber Mafia.* New York: Little, Brown, 2021.

Gordin, Michael, and G. John Ikenberry, eds. *The Age of Hiroshima.* Princeton, NJ: Princeton University Press, 2020.

Griffiths, Owen. "Need, Greed, and Protest in Japan's Black Market." *Journal of Social History* 35 (2002): 825–58.

Groves, Leslie. *Now It Can Be Told: The Story of the Manhattan Project.* New York: Harper & Row, 1962.

Grunow, Tristan. "A Reexamination of the 'Shock of Hiroshima': The Japanese Bomb Projects and Surrender Reconsidered." *Journal of American-East Asian Relations* 12, nos. 3–4 (2003): 155–89.

Guillain, Robert. *I Saw Tokyo Burning: An Eyewitness Narrative from Pearl Harbor to Hiroshima.* New York: Doubleday, 1981.

Guillaume, Marine. "Napalm in U.S. Bombing Doctrine and Practice, 1942–1975." *Asia-Pacific Journal: Japan Focus* 14, no. 23 (2016): 1–3.

Hansell, Haywood. *The Strategic Air War Against Germany and Japan.* Washington, DC: Office of Air Force History, 1986.

Hatano Sumio. "The Atomic Bomb and Soviet Entry into the War: Of Equal Importance." In *The End of the Pacific War: Reappraisals*, edited by Tsuyoshi Hasegawa, chap. 3. Stanford, CA: Stanford University Press, 2007.

Havens, Thomas. *Valley of Darkness: The Japanese People and World War II.* New York: Norton, 1978.

Hibiki Yamaguchi, Fumihiko Yoshida, and Radomir Compel. "Can the Atomic Bombings on Japan Be Justified? A Conversation with Dr. Tsuyoshi Hasegawa." *Journal of Peace and Nuclear Disarmament* 2, no. 1 (2019): 19–33.

Holloway, David. "Jockeying for Position in the Postwar World." In *The End of the Pacific War: Reappraisals*, edited by Tsuyoshi Hasegawa, chap. 5. Stanford, CA: Stanford University Press, 2007.

Huston, John, ed. *American Air Power Comes of Age: General Henry "Hap" Arnold's World War II Diaries: Volume 2*. Maxwell, AL: Air University Press, 2002.

Ichikawa Hiroo. "Reconstructing Tokyo: The Attempt to Transform the Metropolis." In *Rebuilding Urban Japan After 1945*, edited by Carola Hein, Jeffry Diefendorf, and Ichida Yorifusa, chap. 3. Basingstoke, UK: Palgrave Macmillan, 2003.

Janssens, Rudolf. *"What Future for Japan": U.S. Wartime Planning for the Postwar Era, 1942–43*. Amsterdam: University of Amsterdam, 1995.

Johnston, Bruce. *Japanese Food Management in World War II*. Stanford, CA: Stanford University Press, 1953.

Karacas, Cary. "Place, Public Memory, and the Tokyo Air Raid." *Geographical Review* 100, no. 4 (2010): 521–37.

Kase Toshikazu. *Eclipse of the Rising Sun*. London: Jonathan Cape, 1951.

Kawamura Noriko. *Emperor Hirohito and the Pacific War*. Seattle: University of Washington Press, 2015.

Kazuyo Yamane. "Current Attitudes to the Atomic Bombing of Japan." *Medicine, Conflict, and Survival* 11, no. 3 (1995): 46–54.

Kelly, Jason. "Why Did Henry Stimson Spare Kyoto from the Bomb? Confusion in Postwar Historiography." *Journal of American-East Asian Relations* 19, no. 2 (2012): 183–203.

Kozak, Warren. *LeMay: The Life and Wars of General Curtis LeMay*. Washington, DC: Regnery, 2009.

Krebs, Gerhard. "Operation Super-Sunrise? Japanese-United States Peace Feelers in Switzerland, 1945." *Journal of Military History* 69 (2005): 1081–1120.

Laurence, William. *Dawn over Zero: The Story of the Atomic Bomb*. New York: Knopf, 1946.

LeMay, Curtis, and MacKinlay Kantor. *Mission with LeMay: My Story*. New York: Doubleday, 1965.

Levidis, Andrew. "The War Is Not Over: Kishi Nobusuke and the National Defense Brotherhood, 1944–45." *Journal of Japanese Studies* 49, no. 1 (2023): 1–30.

Libby, Justin. "The Search for a Negotiated Peace: Japanese Diplomats' Attempt to Surrender Prior to the Bombing of Hiroshima and Nagasaki." *World Affairs* 156, no. 1 (1993): 35–45.

MacEachin, Douglas. *The Final Months of the War with Japan: Signals Intelligence, U.S. Planning, and the A-Bomb Decision.* Washington, DC: Center for the Study of Intelligence, 1998.

Malloy, Sean. *Atomic Tragedy: Henry L. Stimson and the Decision to Use the Bomb Against Japan.* Ithaca, NY: Cornell University Press, 2008.

———. "'The Rules of Civilized Warfare': Scientists, Civilians, and American Nuclear Strategy, 1940–1945." *Journal of Strategic Studies* 30, no. 3 (2007): 475–512.

Masahiko Yamabe. "Thinking Now About the Great Tokyo Air Raid." *Asia-Pacific Journal: Japan Focus* 9, no. 3 (2011): 1–5.

Matray, James. "Potsdam Revisited: Prelude to a Divided Korea." *Journal of American-East Asian Relations* 24 (2017): 259–82.

Matsumara, Janice. "Internal Security in Wartime Japan (1937–45) and the Creation of Internal Insecurity." *Canadian Journal of History* 31, no. 3 (1996): 395–412.

McMeekin, Sean. *Stalin's War.* London: Allen Lane, 2021.

Miller, Edward. *War Plan Orange: The U.S. Strategy to Defeat Japan 1897–1945.* Annapolis, MD: Naval Institute Press, 1991.

Miscamble, Wilson. *The Most Controversial Decision: Truman, the Atom Bomb, and the Defeat of Japan.* Cambridge: Cambridge University Press, 2011.

Mohan, Uday, and Sanho Tree. "Hiroshima, the American Media, and the Construction of Conventional Wisdom." *Journal of American-East Asian Relations* 4, no. 2 (1995): 141–60.

Monk, Ray. *Inside the Circle: The Life of J. Robert Oppenheimer.* London: Jonathan Cape, 2012.

Moon, John van Courtland. "Project SPHINX: The Question of the Use of Gas in the Planned Invasion of Japan." *Journal of Strategic Studies* 12, no. 3 (1989): 303–23.

Moore, Aaron. *Bombing the City: Civilian Accounts of the Air War in Britain and Japan, 1939–1945.* Cambridge: Cambridge University Press, 2018.

Nagai Takashi. *We of Nagasaki.* London: Gollancz, 1951.

Nicholas, H. G., ed. *Washington Despatches, 1944–45: Weekly Political Reports from the British Embassy.* London: Weidenfeld & Nicolson, 1981.

O'Brien, Phillips. "The Joint Chiefs of Staff, the Atom Bomb, the American Military Mind, and the End of the Second World War." *Journal of Strategic Studies* 42, no. 7 (2019): 971–91.

Overy, Richard. *The Bombing War: Europe 1939–1945.* London: Allen Lane, 2013.

———. "The 'Weak Link'? The Perception of the German Working Class by RAF Bomber Command, 1940–1945." *Labour History Review* 77, no. 1 (2012): 11–34.

Park, W. Hays. "'Precision and Area Bombing': Who Did Which, and When?" *Journal of Strategic Studies* 18, no. 1 (1995): 145–74.

Paur, Erich. "The Broken Axis—8 May 1945 in Japan." In *Japan and Germany*, vol. 1, edited by Akira Kudō, Tajima Nobuo, and Erich Pauer, 530–50. Leiden: Brill, 2009.

Pike, Francis. *Hirohito's War: The Pacific War 1941–1945.* London: Bloomsbury, 2015.

Plung, Dylan. "The Impact of Urban Evacuation in Japan During World War II." *Asia-Pacific Journal: Japan Focus* 19, no. 1 (2021): 5–9.

———. "The Japanese Village at Dugway Proving Ground: An Unexamined Context to the Firebombing of Japan." *Asia-Pacific Journal: Japan Focus* 16, no. 8 (2018): 1–5.

Porter, Patrick. "Paper Bullets: American Psywar in the Pacific, 1944–1945." *War in History* 17, no. 4 (2010): 479–511.

Ralph, William. "Improvised Destruction: Arnold, LeMay, and the Firebombing of Japan." *War in History* 13, no. 4 (2006): 495–522.

Rhodes, Richard. *The Making of the Atomic Bomb.* New York: Simon & Schuster, 1986.

Roberts, Geoffrey. *Stalin's Wars from World War Two to Cold War, 1939–1945.* New Haven, CT: Yale University Press, 2006.

Rotter, Andrew. *Hiroshima: The World's Bomb.* Oxford: Oxford University Press, 2008.

Saburō Ienya. *The Pacific War 1931–1945.* New York: Random House, 1978.

Sarantakas, Nicholas. "The Royal Air Force on Okinawa: The Diplomacy of a Coalition on the Verge of Victory." *Diplomatic History* 27, no. 4 (2003): 479–502.

———. "Warriors of Word and Sword: The Battle of Okinawa, Media

Coverage, and Truman's Reevaluation of Strategy in the Pacific." *Journal of American-East Asian Relations* 23–24 (2016): 334–67.

Schwabe, David. *Burning Japan: Air Force Bombing Strategy Change in the Pacific*. Lincoln, NE: Potomac Books, 2015.

Scott, James. *Black Snow: Curtis LeMay, The Firebombing of Tokyo, and the Road to the Atomic Bomb*. New York: Norton, 2022.

Shillony, Ben-Ami. *Politics and Culture in Wartime Japan*. Oxford: Oxford University Press, 1981.

Sigal, Leon. *Fighting to the Finish: The Politics of War Termination in the United States and Japan, 1945*. Ithaca, NY: Cornell University Press, 1988.

Snow, Philip. *China & Russia: Four Centuries of Conflict and Concord*. New Haven, CT: Yale University Press, 2023.

Szasz, Ferenc. *British Scientists and the Manhattan Project: The Los Alamos Years*. London: Macmillan, 1992.

———. "'Pamphlets Away': The Allied Propaganda Campaign over Japan During the Last Months of World War II." *Journal of Popular Culture* 42, no. 3 (2009): 530–40.

Takafusa Nakamura and Konosuke Odaka, eds. *Economic History of Japan, 1914–1945*. Oxford: Oxford University Press, 1999.

Thorpe, Charles. "Against Time: Scheduling, Momentum, and Moral Order at Wartime Los Alamos." *Journal of Historical Sociology* 17, no. 1 (2004): 31–55.

Truman, Harry S. *Year of Decision, 1945: The Memoirs of Harry S. Truman, Volume I*. London: Hodder & Stoughton, 1955.

Uchiyama, Benjamim. *Japan's Carnival War: Mass Culture on the Home Front, 1937–1945*. Cambridge: Cambridge University Press, 2018.

Walker, J. Samuel. *Prompt and Utter Destruction: Truman and the Use of the Atomic Bomb Against Japan*. Chapel Hill: University of North Carolina Press, 2016.

Walsh, Brian. "Japanese Foreign Ministry Document Destruction Order of 7 August 1945." *Journal of American-East Asian Relations* 26 (2009): 85–94.

Weale, Adrian, ed. *Hiroshima: First-Hand Accounts of the Atomic Terror That Changed the World*. London: Robinson Publishing, 1995.

Weisenfeld, Gennifer. *Gas Mask Nation: Visualizing Civil Air Defense in Wartime Japan*. Chicago: University of Chicago Press, 2023.

Werrell, Kenneth. *Blankets of Fire: U.S. Bombers over Japan During World War II.* Washington, DC: Smithsonian Press, 1996.

Yamashita, Samuel. *Daily Life in Wartime Japan 1940–1945.* Lawrence: University of Kansas Press, 2015.

Yellen, Jeremy. "The Specter of Revolution: Reconsidering Japan's Decision to Surrender." *International History Review* 35, no. 1 (2013): 205–26.

Yukiko Koshiro. "Eurasian Eclipse: Japan's End Game in World War II." *American Historical Review* 109, no. 2 (2004): 417–44.

Yuko Matsunari and Nao Yoshimoto. "Comparison of Rescue and Relief Activities Within 72 Hours of the Atomic Bombings in Hiroshima and Nagasaki." *Prehospital and Disaster Medicine* 28, no. 6 (2013): 536–42.

Zwigenberg, Ran. *Hiroshima: The Origins of a Global Memory Culture.* Cambridge: Cambridge University Press, 2014.

Index